'This book makes a vital co[ntribution] conversation. There is a prophe[tic] new kinds of leadership teams and developed. These leaders ne[ed] [partnerships] forged across cultures from different ethnic churches. The goal, says Kumbi, is to plant multi-ethnic churches which are led by a cross-section of culturally diverse leaders in order to represent the multicultural diversity of the kingdom of God. The multicultural tapestry of the West means the world is on our doorstep. In order to represent the power of the Spirit of Christ to unite peoples in their diversity, we need to equip, train and mentor leaders who can work together in culturally intelligent ways to help establish these fresh expressions of church.'

Rev Dr Andy Hardy, Undergraduate Programme Director, ForMission College

'This is a must read for any leaders who are grappling with how indigenous and ethnic churches engage in mission in multicultural contexts. The book pulls no punches in identifying key issues, such as the default tendency towards monoculturalism in migrant and white churches, often making them irrelevant to their local communities.

'It particularly challenges leaders to discover a new vision of what a multicultural church community could be like, and calls on them to think outside the box and work creatively together with others from different ethnicities. Hirpo Kumbi writes with passion and great insight, reflecting his experience and thorough research. This book is very timely in the current social and political climate; it offers hope and clear direction for the future.'

Paul Lancaster, Founder of Hope for the Nations (Leeds) and Interact (Institute of Intercultural Learning and Action)

'In *The Culturally Intelligent Leader*, Hirpo Kumbi presents a compelling vision of multi-ethnic communities that is at once stirring and realistic. Drawing on his own extensive experience and successful track record in church planting, he gives a sober articulation of the problems and challenges, then proceeds to chart possible pathways towards workable solutions. Starting from a clear theological foundation he interweaves theory with practice. Here we find a realistic and comprehensive analysis of the special issues faced by multi-ethnic leadership teams and practical strategies for working through those issues. His very helpful sections on reverse mission and mentoring address matters of sustainability for the vision, completing a most valuable handbook for every missional leader working in today's multicultural environment.'

Rick Lewis, Anamcara Consulting, Sydney, Australia

'It is paramount for all forms of Christian leadership to be aware of the new paradigms of mission and ministry that continue to shape the 21st century. The old Christendom mission narratives of the West to the rest continue to crumble, thus providing opportunities for us to appropriate new, fresh expressions of missional partnerships.

'This equally affords us the privilege to welcome and engage with various key missional leaders from the majority world. As my dear friend and colleague, I believe that Hirpo is one of these key leaders. He has willingly embraced and developed a reverse mission paradigm and then taught other leaders to follow. It has been a privilege to observe him model the kind of cultural intelligence he expresses within this text.

'This important, timely and prophetic work seeks to foster a way of enabling, challenging, provoking, and retooling this new generation of leadership who continue to arrive and

The Culturally Intelligent Leader

Developing Multi-ethnic Communities in a Multicultural Age

Hirpo Kumbi

instant
apostle

First published in Great Britain in 2017

Instant Apostle

The Barn
1 Watford House Lane
Watford
Herts
WD17 1BJ

Every effort has been made to seek permission to use copyright material reproduced in this book. The publisher apologises for those cases where permission might not have been sought and, if notified, will formally seek permission at the earliest opportunity.

The views and opinions expressed in this work are those of the author and do not necessarily reflect the views and opinions of the publisher.

British Library Cataloguing-in-Publication Data

A catalogue record for this book is available from the British Library

This book and all other Instant Apostle books are available from Instant Apostle:

Website: www.instantapostle.com

E-mail: info@instantapostle.com

ISBN 978-1-909728-73-8

Printed in Great Britain

To my son, Matiel Hirpo, from whom I have learnt much about the joy of living, and who is also a third-culture kid.

Acknowledgements

There are people who have helped me to make *The Culturally Intelligent Leader* a reality. In particular, my heartfelt appreciation and thanks go to Dr Richard Whitehouse, Dr Clement Katulushi, Rev Dr Andy Hardy and Mr Bob Straddling for sharing their time generously and aspirations with me in this journey.

I am also grateful to Rev Dr Rick Lewes, Rev Dan Yarnell, Paul Lancaster and Dr Harvey Kwiyani for their commendations.

Finally, I wish to express my deepest thanks to Dr Martin Robinson for contributing a foreword.

About the Author

Hirpo is originally from Ethiopia, where he was a business entrepreneur from a very young age. He became a Christian in his early twenties. He joined the Orthodox Reformation movement, now known as Emmanuel United Church of Ethiopia, in the town of Arsi Negele, where he served as an elder in charge of deacons and external relationships. He also planted a church before coming to the UK in late 2002.

In the UK, he planted churches in Leeds and Sheffield, called Emmanuel Christian Fellowship UK Cities, and supported other new church plants through which he connected with the Fellowship of the Churches of Christ (FCC). Today, Hirpo is part of the National Leadership Team for the FCC. Hirpo is a graduate in Missional Leadership from the University of Wales.

He is also currently part of the ForMission College Senior Management Team and has the specific role of Director of Operations, which sees him engaging with different campuses all over the country.

Hirpo has served ForMission College in a number of roles. He was Campus Director for Leeds before taking on the responsibility of Regional Director for the North Region, covering Leeds, Manchester, Liverpool and the Intensive Campus. He was also Module Leader for Reverse Mission with teaching responsibilities in Leadership in

Missional Ministry for different year groups. Hirpo has sat on the Board of Trustees of ForMission College for the past four years. Prior to joining ForMission College, Hirpo worked as an accountant.

He is passionate about mission, especially church planting, and training leaders for mission. Hirpo is a frequent speaker for a TV channel known as El Shaddai Amharic TV Network. He regularly undertakes mission trips to Ethiopia as well as to other European countries for leadership training with Ethiopian communities.

Contents

Foreword

We sometimes forget that the modern missionary movement was born at a time when the church in the West did not feel that it was making an impact on society. The church felt weak and ineffective. To some extent, the intention of the missionary movement was to create a strong church in other parts of the world that would ultimately help the church in the West overcome the indifference towards God that had been a strong feature of eighteenth-century life in Europe and America. One writer from the period calls this 'the blessed reflex'. The dream of mission from everywhere to everywhere was deeply imbedded in the very first impetus of the modern missionary movement.

Ironically, after the launch of the modern missionary movement, the church started to make more impact in the Western world, before 'the blessed reflex' could begin to operate. The very success of the nineteenth-century church in strengthening Christian witness at home caused the missionary movement to become identified with mission from the West to the rest. It has proved to be very difficult to create a different script even today when, in reality, more mission comes to the West from the rest than the other way round.

There are many reasons why this is so. Cross-cultural mission is a difficult skill to attain, and, frankly, not many are gifted in this area. That is why most African, Asian and South American mission efforts in the West end up evangelising people from their own nation, language group or ethnicity. Very few succeed in crossing cultural boundaries.

Intercultural mission leading to multi-ethnic communities, where leaders from a variety of cultures manage to create an international church or fellowship, are also rare experiences. Again, the skills needed to produce this kind of missionary or church encounter are not easy to acquire and practice. Yet it is precisely this kind of mission that is urgently needed in the present multicultural context of the West.

At the very moment when 'the blessed reflex' dreamed of by the first missionaries is actually present among us, we do not seem able to use the amazing resources that the arrival of Christians from other lands offers to us. The book that follows is specifically designed to encourage the development of significant intercultural mission.

The author, Hirpo Kumbi, is a gifted practitioner of mission, an able church planter and a leader who has deeply understood the importance of empowering others. Hirpo has understood the complexity involved in preparing leaders for the enterprise of intercultural mission. And it is a multifaceted process.

The book covers a wide range of topics, beginning wisely with the challenges of leadership and then covering issues that few books in this area tackle. I particularly applaud the concept of cultural intelligence. It is not enough to know a language. Cultural sensitivity involves a special gift of grace. The following pages are full of practical wisdom, especially when it comes to guidance for those who wish to be first-generation 'reverse missionaries'.

This is a book that is inspired by actual experience. In that sense it both contains theory and operates as a practitioner's guide. It is full of real-life examples and illustrations. I particularly applaud the chapters on the second- and third-generation children of African leaders.

The chapter on the importance of mentoring has a special significance in this context, given the wide range of meanings that Africans in particular ascribe to the word 'mentor'. The idea of mutuality in mentoring is especially precious and deserving of close attention.

The presence of huge numbers of Christians from other lands in the West presents us with a moment of immense opportunity. The Christian community has the opportunity to model in a practical way what it means to be a multicultural society.

This is not about strengthening the church, however helpful that might be, so much as becoming a sign and foretaste of the gospel itself, pointing as it does to a new society. In becoming, jointly, citizens of heaven and wanderers in the world, paradoxically we demonstrate how to become prophetic citizens here on earth. By having a heavenly vision, we know better how to create a more fulfilled earthly world.

You will enjoy absorbing these pages, not just reading the words but also ingesting the vision.

Dr Martin Robinson, author; Principal of ForMission College

Preface

The world today is rapidly changing as globalisation has developed into a much more visible reality, thanks to advances in information and computing technology, transport, travel and the way societies interact. Even a small village in the remotest part of the planet is likely to be connected to the rest of the world by some form of communication. Very few parts of the world are yet untouched by Western influences, and in those parts where change has been fully embraced, challenges remain at various levels, including the cultural and missional level. Missional communities are faced with fresh questions about mission in unfamiliar contexts, including reaching unchurched emergent generations, as well as those disconnected because of the missional legacy of their parents.

In the UK, there is a multiplicity of diverse cultural expressions of missional communities. For example, there are missional communities engaged in reverse mission that is full of passion for mission, driven by gospel fervour, wanting to reach all areas of British society. Then there is the host British culture and its missional churches, which are often uncertain about how to relate to the new people groups settling down among them. This is to a significant extent because of limited understanding of how to communicate with those who come from a world culture different to a Western one. Situations like these not only beg questions, but also invite responses. However, it is not the case that there are no reference points from which answers and examples might be found to show how we might move forward.

Among the sources that may be mined in order to support missional churches of any subcultural background in the West is a significant body of literature on world cultures and anthropological work that has been carried out by missionaries. A significant writer in this field is the late Paul Hiebert. He taught and wrote copiously on the subject of the gospel, mission and culture.[1] His work can help those interested in developing their understanding of world cultures significantly.

In this book, I will discuss the need for leaders and members of emerging multi-ethnic and multicultural churches to develop their understanding of other cultures. I follow Livermore's groundbreaking work in the field of cultural intelligence (the abbreviation CQ will be used to represent the phrase cultural quotient). Later in the book the need to develop cultural intelligence will be addressed. Although a full analysis of CQ is not offered here, reference points to others' work in this field are provided.[2] We do not live in a monoculture, but in a multicultural society, and all of us will have to adapt. However, we can be encouraged

---

[1] P Hiebert, *The Gospel in Human Contexts: Anthropological Explorations for Contexts* (Grand Rapids, MI: Baker Academic, 2009).

[2] A Hardy and D Yarnell, *Forming Multicultural Partnerships: Church Planting in a Divided Society* (Watford: Instant Apostle, 2015).

that Jesus was a Jew from a Jewish monoculture, but with a mission that was broader, just as it is for His Church today.

The New Testament account of Jesus explains that Jesus started His mission within a monocultural setting (Israel) with the ultimate goal of fulfilling a multinational, multicultural mission. Jesus gathered a team of potential leaders and, during His time with them, offered Himself as the perfect model of leadership. He not only trained the leaders, but He was also their mentor.

After a while, Jesus commissioned His immediate disciples to preach and to demonstrate the kingdom of God through healing and exorcism, thus meeting two of the most pressing social needs of His day. He sent them out in twos, and during this time they exercised those skills they had learned, acquired and developed during their time with Him.

According to Luke, Jesus later sent out another seventy-two followers charged with the same task. When they reported back to Him, He rejoiced that the outcome signalled the defeat of Satan. This indicates that the missional task was not to be confined to the original twelve apostles, but was to be shared more widely; a task that began to be fulfilled with the birth of the Church at Pentecost. Church planting formed an important part of the process of announcing the kingdom or reign of God, as it is to this day.

Kingdom community growth was something the new leaders experienced after Jesus had left them. The book of Acts demonstrates that the post-Pentecost Church was to be made up of a broad tableau of cultures that made up the

Greco–Roman Empire. Under the guidance and authority of the Holy Spirit, the leaders saw the Church grow among these multiple cultural groups. This experience brought with it new challenges, which included a level of tension and conflict.

Intercultural conflicts can also easily arise, and it is important to consider how to develop and apply cultural intelligence to minimise these issues. In Acts, the leaders learned to deal with the controversy inevitably involved in establishing, at times, what were multicultural communities, and so must we.

Why was it necessary for Jesus to start His mission within a monocultural context? One possible answer is that when in the beginning God created one *person*, He ultimately had one *people* in mind. However, the Genesis 11 narrative tells us that this one people scattered throughout the world, resulting in the formation of many cultures with many different languages. The book of Ephesians clearly states that Jesus came to create one community that would be united in Him. So while Jesus may have begun His mission in a predominantly monocultural setting, it was never meant to be limited to this.

Both Peter and Paul's writings, as well as the book of Revelation, indicate that part of God's plan in reversing the consequences of the fall of humankind is to include all people in His restored heaven on earth. Thus, rather than merely going back to a monocultural Eden, God intends to bring in the cultural riches and diversity of every nation and language to enhance worship before His throne. In our current context in Britain, the reality is that there are various cultures and diverse nationalities in many cities and towns, which make up what might be termed 'the world on our doorstep'. The leadership example of Jesus and the early Church is meant to address the necessity of reaching all peoples, not just one group. Their example embraces the breadth of God's redemptive purpose.

In this book, I start by looking at leadership as an essential element in developing multi-ethnic missional communities, and then go on to consider how the move from single cultures to a multi-ethnic cultural context constitutes a *Kairos* moment in missions. The effectiveness of multicultural communities for mission depends to a large extent upon the character qualities and intercultural skills of their leaders. These qualities and skills go hand in hand: in the multicultural setting, the missional leader recognises the need for both and that they are interdependent. The fruitfulness of their intercultural skills depends upon their personal, character qualities, and without the intercultural skills their character qualities will be missed. Consequently, qualities and skills are related and necessary in the leading and developing of multi-ethnic communities for mission.

A significant part of this book centres on 'reverse mission' and related factors, such as the outlook of first-generation missionaries and the challenge faced by their third culture children, and conflict management. Reverse mission is a phenomenon where people in those nations outside the West who were first reached by Western Christian missionaries, now themselves having a strong Christian presence, aspire to bring the gospel back to the countries from where it first came to them. In short, the

West is seen as a mission field in reverse to be re-evangelised.

The last two chapters recognise that there is need to mentor leaders from immigrant churches, with a particular study of and appreciation of the African experience and perspective, as well as focusing on cross-cultural partnerships that help all missional leaders of every culture to journey together. The process of mentoring is necessary, given the fact that missional leadership is complex and not meant to be a solitary burden.

This sequence or ordering of the material follows the structure given in the New Testament. It is moving on from developing a team of leaders, just as Christ did, and then empowering and equipping them to develop multi-ethnic, and often multinational, communities for mission.

Part One

Leadership

Chapter One

Multi-ethnic Leadership

A prerequisite for developing any form of society, community or team is leadership. Leaders are crucial in any context, including the multi-ethnic missional community. The nature and form of any grouping or coming together of different people, from basic units to complex societies, begins with leadership often invested in one individual, who attracts and draws others, and together they articulate a vision and exercise authority to realise that vision. Today's multicultural, multi-ethnic communities pose more challenges than the predominantly monocultural, mono-ethnic communities of the past, and a multicultural, multi-ethnic leadership style is the key to meeting these new demands.

Visiting a local church one day, I was struck by the composition of the congregation. This church is a beautiful sight since there are more than 600 members, with at least thirty nationalities represented within the congregation. This picture looks good. It is a situation to be desired, when different people come together from different nations and gather in one place as disciples of Christ. It seems to represent the realisation of the kingdom of God. However, in this multinational congregation, the leadership consisted of an all-white British team of four. This small team had taken upon itself the task of leading such a large church made up of people from different cultures and nationalities. The leaders foster the only culture they are familiar with: their British culture. The style of worship, the clothes worn or dress codes, the language, the food, all these are the norms the other twenty-nine nationalities implicitly adhere to. Non-white British members of this multinational, multicultural and multi-ethnic congregation do not seem to be part of the core team exercising spiritual gifts of leadership because of the monocultural leadership style of the church.

A situation where a monocultural leadership is in charge of a multicultural congregation is fundamentally flawed because it fails to acknowledge the multicultural nature of authority of the missional community. I mention this visit as an example, but having lived in Europe for the past fifteen years I have observed that this is common in many church settings. The big issue is that host churches are often knowingly or unknowingly failing to recognise and accept the gifts of other potential leaders so that they struggle to become effective missionally. The roles given to ethnic leaders may not relate to their spiritual gifts and seem to fall under activities such as leading a small group or ushering. Despite the fact that these roles are also a respected part of ministry, they do not fully release the gifts of many people.

In order to exercise their gifts more fully, many of these leaders then break out to plant churches among their own communities. This seems to be a good and worthy venture, as they are still converting people to Christ. However, what is happening here is that the host church leaders and ethnic leaders are both following the same style of leadership – reaching out to their own monocultural background. Inadvertently, both host culture churches and immigrant church leaders are contributing to division in God's mission when they are supposed to synergise.

The following table illustrates observations about missional communities in the UK today:

Church type	Aspiration	Reality
White British (host culture)	• Provide a welcome • Provide support to immigrants • Involve and include migrants (ie non-British) • Include migrants in leadership • Recognise multiplicity of ethnicities in worship • Integrate the next generation	• Immigrant congregations often end up providing a welcome • Provide a worship space for ethnic congregation, charge rent • Slow integration at best • Cautious approach is often adopted • Monocultural even when congregation has multiple ethnicities present • Unsure where the next generation belongs

Immigrant church	• Reach host nation • White indigenous people and other nationalities to join • Grow and plant more churches • Become full British, corporate church • Integrate the next generation	• Do not know how: trial and error rather than training • Similar ethnic membership: black Africans attract black Africans • Growth by birth not conversion • Desire to maintain unique cultural identity • Unsure where the next generation belongs

In the table above, the aspirations of both host culture and immigrant churches are challenged by reality. The concept of the multi-ethnic missional community is embraced by both indigenous British churches and immigrant churches, but the reality is that this has not been achieved yet by either types of church in the UK. The way forward is partly through missional leadership conversations in which the gift of multi-ethnic leaders to the church is embraced. The conversations can seek to explore opportunities for meeting the needs of both types of churches.

The current situation

In most European countries today, many host culture churches complain about immigrant-led churches, saying that they still operate using an exclusivist Christian language that is not understood by those outside their faith communities. This is true, to a large extent. However, it is also true that many host culture churches are not as welcoming as they could be. For example, two of my students wanted to change their church membership from a black African congregation to a white British congregation. However, one of the host culture church members redirected the black family to an African church, despite the fact that this family had made a deliberate decision to seek to join this white congregation. In another case, someone was sent to a different mission agency because of their ethnicity rather than having their leadership potential, qualities and skills embraced by the church they were currently attending.

These examples show how the importance of multi-ethnic leadership and partnership to mission has not been understood. A few years ago, a more significant example saw an ethnic, immigrant church being asked to leave a host monoculture church's premises when it sought to reshape its own African monoculture worship after the pattern of host culture worship, which it was seeking the support of the host culture church to do. The church believed that this would enhance its next generation missional engagement with the hosting culture and other nationalities in the neighbourhoods. By causing the immigrant church to vacate their premises and thus curtail the partnership, the host church in effect undermined the missional strategy of the immigrant church. The action of the host church asking the immigrant church to leave and to stop using their building set this new church back by several months. The stated reason was that the host church needed to use all its space! This setback affected the immigrant church's missional desire and impeded its strategy towards becoming a multi-ethnic congregation in partnership with the host culture church itself. A wonderful opportunity to partner together and learn from one another was lost.

There are a few UK missionary denominations that support immigrant churches being planted here. This is positive in terms of maintaining the original and often historical connection with the sending country, and also offers the immigrant churches support through common events or conferences. Yet even in these instances, so little is achieved. The historic missionary-connected churches that have been planted in the UK also end up as monoculture churches, whose members come from the former mission field.

A quick browse of the websites of a few of these missionary denominations reveals how ethnic separation still exists in the leadership make-up. One such denomination has a nine-strong, all-white leadership team with responsibility for the entire UK. When the leadership of these organisations is not multi-ethnic, is it any wonder that the churches they plant do not succeed in crossing ethnic boundaries either?

However, not all missional organisations are the same. The Fellowship of Churches of Christ in Great Britain and

Ireland (FCC), for example, is a network of churches that embraces Christian leaders from multiple ethnic backgrounds as part of its national leadership team. The efforts of the FCC are to be commended. It seeks to enable leaders by adopting a non-denominational Christian theology and encourages migrants to assume leadership positions.

There are also examples of some mainstream churches embracing the grace of multi-ethnic leadership. The Church of England has appointed Archbishop John Sentamu, who was originally from Uganda, as Archbishop of York. This followed the earlier ordination of Michael Nazir-Ali as Bishop of Rochester. He is a Pakistani leader who was formerly the General Secretary of the Anglican Church Missionary Society, and though now retired, he is still active in promoting multicultural mission. The Baptist Union has welcomed and appointed ethnic minority church leaders, and the Methodist Church in the UK also has a policy of promoting such leaders.[3] In the worlds of business and sport, large boardrooms are increasingly revealing multi-ethnic leadership patterns, such as FIFA, the ICC and Microsoft, and the Church needs to follow suit.

In the case of immigrant missionaries, it can be difficult to take the lead in establishing multi-ethnic partnerships, owing to practical constraints. To begin with, limited

---

[3] See the paper written by Brazilian Methodist missionary in the UK, Oseias da Silva, 'Reverse mission in the Western context', available at www.wesley.cam.ac.uk/holiness (accessed 22nd May 2017); *HOLINESS: The Journal of Wesley House Cambridge*, Volume I (2015) Issue 2, pp231-244.

financial and physical resources or assets seriously affect not only their missional scope but also their 'weight' in prospective partnerships. In addition to the lack of resources, they are likely to be neglected even by local authorities when seeking to access public funding and resources. Often, immigrant churches are subject to political restrictions, since they exercise no civic influence in comparison with their host culture counterparts. Mainstream churches or host culture churches generally have an established infrastructure and the financial resources to back up their vision, but this also tends to give them a dominant role in any partnership with immigrant churches.

This truth needs to be addressed if we are to establish genuine multi-ethnic, multicultural missional leadership. Meeting the needs of immigrant churches is a partnership opportunity for the host culture church. The combination of the infrastructure and resources available to host culture churches with the calling of reverse missionaries or immigrant churches can spur on the development of true multi-ethnic communities.

Theological underpinning for multi-ethnic leadership

The formation of leaders needs to be underpinned by a biblical and theological basis, or rationale, for their vocation. The story of Abraham in the Old Testament reveals a specific calling to Abraham, who was an early recipient of the gospel, in the sense that he believed God's promise of an heir and his faith was credited to him as righteousness. This foreshadowed salvation in Christ, and Abraham was thus called to be the father of nations.

The seven deacons in Acts 6 are multinational, with names suggesting Hellenistic or Greek-speaking Jewish backgrounds, including Nicolas, who was a Gentile convert to Judaism. These are called to a wider audience than the Jewish community only.

Another example is Paul, whose mission team included Luke, a full-blooded Gentile, and Timothy, half-Jewish on his mother's side and Greek on his father's side. Paul had him circumcised to remove cultural barriers between him and full Jews, not because it was necessary for salvation. Paul himself was called to be an apostle, to bear Jesus' name before Gentiles and kings (Romans 1:1; 11:13; Ephesians 3:8-9; Acts 9:15). Paul was from Tarsus and was educated under Gamaliel, a Jerusalem rabbi.

Besides Paul, the church at Antioch in Acts 13 had a leadership team which was made up of Hellenistic Jews, including Barnabas from Cyprus, some Greeks, and Lucius, a North African from Cyrene, as well as Simeon who was called Niger (meaning he was black) from Africa.

The multinational, multi-ethnic nature of leadership is evident from the very conception of mission. In each of the examples mentioned above, the elect have a calling, the end of which in God's plan is a multi-ethnic society. Israel, as a nation, is ultimately not meant to be inward-looking. The calling of Israel was to be a kingdom of priests declaring God's praises (Exodus 19:6). In this sense, the role of Israel as priests was in turn to be a blessing to many nations.

The multinational purpose of God is a theme running not only in the lives of key biblical figures, but also in the history and election of an entire nation. As Peter said, God has chosen for Himself a people, a royal priesthood, a holy nation (1 Peter 2:9). Therefore, to be authentic in developing a multinational and multicultural community, the multi-ethnic leadership model is key.

Leadership development

In a culturally and ethnically diverse setting, a missional leader needs the ability to recognise and then mobilise resources already present within the community. These resources may be natural or spiritual. In both cases, the leader needs to be able to recognise the gifts and skills that their people have. In a multi-ethnic community, there is the possibility that the leader will have access to a much larger pool of resources made even richer in their diversity, scope and depth. This means that the ability to recognise these resources demands from the leader a heightened level of alertness, a keenness to spot new gifting while having the sensitivity to refresh already known gifts. In addition to recognising natural skills, the leader needs to be able to discern spiritual gifts by their knowledge of Scripture and by revelation from the Holy Spirit. As theologian Philip Greenslade states, 'Revelation is vital to leadership. God's view of things, not man's view.'[4]

At this point it is worth observing that in my fifteen or so years of leadership in churches, I have noticed that some

---

[4] Philip Greenslade, *Leadership: A Biblical Pattern for Today* (London: Marshall, Morgan & Scott, 1984), p44.

people aspire to leadership who neither have the character traits nor the aptitude that match their aspirations. Such people can become divisive if a suitable role within the body of Christ that fulfils their desire to make a difference is not found for them. They must be brought to see that the desire to make a difference is both worthy and God-given, but does not necessarily make them leaders. People who threaten to create division if they are not given the position they demand are often ego-driven and determined either to conquer or to divide a congregation to get their own way. They do not have the spirit or the mind of Christ and should be dealt with carefully but firmly.

At the same time, leaders can unwittingly collude with an inflated ambition by promoting individuals above their level of competence. In business circles this is known as 'the Peter Principle', the phenomenon where a person rises through application and effort to the top level of their abilities and is then promoted to a position beyond their level of competence, which they cannot sustain. Such people can become a menace both to themselves and to the organisation they purport to serve. This is a management problem that can be tricky to negotiate.

It is also likely to be the case that the multi-ethnic community by nature presents demands on the leader's ability to mobilise the resources possessed by the community. Mobilisation as a task will therefore need skills that can complement the leader's own skills, but be drawn together in such a way that the resources serve the purposes they are intended to meet. The greater the extent and scope of the resources, the greater the responsibility placed upon the leader, and the greater the need for resource mobilisation and management in the multi-ethnic missional community.

Furthermore, it is not enough to recognise the variety of gifts possessed by members of the team; the missional leader needs to instruct them. A training institute, college or other appropriate body should be seriously considered as a necessary ingredient in mission, since leaders cannot do everything on their own. Looking to other trainers helps to provide alternative experiences and views, otherwise the next generation of leaders will draw their experience only from their first teacher, resulting in something akin to cloning.

After discerning and recognising emerging gifts, the leader needs to make sure that these gifts and skills are also recognised by the rest of the multi-ethnic missional community and then released for ministry. As Snyder points out, 'gifts are given for, and in the context of, community'.[5] Gifts are not intended for individual benefit, but for the common good. Gifts are of little use outside the community framework. It is only when these gifts, in their multiplicity and variety, are exploited in serving the multicultural community that their release becomes meaningful.

One way of releasing people's gifts is through apprenticeships, using the same principles as in the workplace. The process will involve some training, after which the apprentice should be given a level of responsibility. The apprentice's progress should be monitored until the role is established. This is nothing new:

[5] Howard A Snyder, *Radical Renewal* (Houston, TX: Touch Publications, 1996), p139.

Jesus used the apprenticeship model in training His disciples. He picked the men He wanted and called them to share His life, He taught them by example as well as by word, and He delegated His authority to them and sent them out to minister in pairs. Then, on their return, He assessed the results with them (Mark 3:13-15; 6:8-12; Luke 10:1-20).

The apprenticeship model can be a stimulating and exciting leadership development feature in the multi-ethnic missional community. As various identities emerge, apprenticeships can impact each level of culture. One culture, the indigenous culture, can train several future leaders from migrant cultures as apprentices. This process is implied when Jesus told the apostles to make disciples of every nation (Matthew 28:18-20): in other words, it is not just a matter of making disciples *from* every nation as much as discipling the culture of whole nations.

As others take part in this ministry, the leader can be released for other ministry functions. In the Old Testament, Moses' father-in-law, Jethro, saw that the burden of leadership was far too heavy. Leaders who prefer to do everything by themselves, like Moses, become over-burdened and stressed. So Jethro suggested that Moses delegate some authority to others (Exodus 18:13-26). Andy Stanley states, 'The secrets of leadership are these: The less you do, the more you accomplish. The less you do, the more you enable others to accomplish.'[6]

Unwillingness to delegate may be caused by pride, insecurity or a desire for efficiency. Some leaders feel it is

---

[6] Andy Stanley, *Next Generation Leader* (Sisters, OR: Multnomah Books, 2003), p17.

easier to do the job themselves. But if it is accepted that people can be empowered, then it follows that people can also grow to the point that they are no longer dependent on the leader, since they come to possess the same strengths as the leader. Mark Twain said that great things can happen when you don't care who gets the credit.[7]

The diagram below represents suggested stages for how to equip a multi-ethnic community to become united:

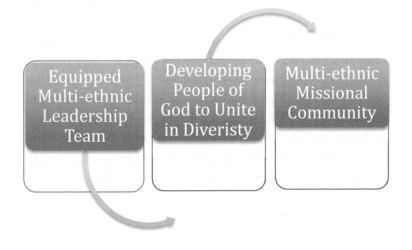

I have argued that churches need leaders who themselves are members of the ethnic communities represented in their multi-ethnic congregations. It is

[7] See http://www.azquotes.com/quote/855738 (accessed 22nd May 2017).

important for leaders from different ethnic and cultural backgrounds to visibly be united as they learn from each other about the different ethnic groups they represent. This really is a first-stage matter of importance. First of all, leaders need to work together in culturally sensitive ways to model this to their communities. Secondly, leaders need to help facilitate intercultural dialogue and fellowship between the different groups in order to help them understand each other's cultural differences, as well as to help them to accept those differences as normal. Over time, the development of a diverse but united multi-ethnic church community should follow. Members will always need to work hard at understanding each other's cultures and what different behaviours mean. However, if they persevere, a community can come to enough maturity for meaningful fellowship to occur across cultural and ethnic lines.

Chapter Two

Catalytic Qualities for Missional Leaders

Leaders who are called into mission are equipped with certain characteristics necessary for participating in the mission of God, the *missio Dei*. The missional leader needs to have vision, passion, commitment and integrity.

Vision

The nature of contemporary society is that communities are not only becoming more culturally diverse, but they are also changing with regard to their ethnic composition. Consequently, a new type of missional leader is needed, one who has the vision and insight into what God is doing now, and who can plan for the future.

In the first instance, such leaders need to be entrepreneurs, people with a vision who are clear about developing multi-ethnic communities. Such leaders are always looking for new ways to reach out to others and expand the work of the church. Good leaders are visionaries with the ability to put their vision into practice. They may not carry out every missional activity themselves but will involve others. As Gibbs observes, 'Church leaders must not only emphasize ministry among the people of God; they also need to mobilize the people of God for mission in the world.'[8]

This mobilisation starts with the leaders themselves. This vision should not be regarded as the leader's personal property; it must be passed on to others by fully involving them and training them to become missional leaders themselves. The vision of the leader is bound to fail if it does not imagine the future, or move to realise that future by the intentional use of creativity, talents or gifting.

Part of the leader's vision is to see the goals and aspirations of the church and to identify the gap between the present and that future. For example, when immigrant churches are planted in the host country, account must be taken of the future of the church. In my experience in pursuing the vision for the churches I have planted, movement towards cultural integration is intentional and real. Churches will become more integrated into the local community sooner or later if they actively seek to do so.

Church networks, such as the Fellowship of Churches of Christ in Great Britain and Ireland, foster relationships between immigrant churches and host culture churches already as part of the shift towards establishing multi-ethnic missional communities. This is part of a process that, in the case of Emanuel Christian Fellowship, UK Cities, will involve a gradual but deliberate transition from using the Amharic language to using English, as members' children grow up and speak English as their first language. This process hinges on the understanding that if this

---

[8] E Gibbs, *Leadership Next* (Leicester: IVP, 2005), p66.

transition does not take place, the church will stagnate and die and the vision will only have been a pipe dream.

The church-planting thinker David Garrison gives the example of a church planting movement among refugees in Holland. After seeing remarkable growth, with more than thirty churches planted in refugee camps, the movement died. The reason was that the refugees moved on and the churches did not adapt to the changing circumstances.[9]

Affiliation with host culture organisations can help with making the transition as it gives opportunity to access resources, including mature people who can offer good advice on integrating with the culture of the host country. Not only do the immigrant churches benefit, but also the indigenous churches and the whole country. However, partnership should not only be 'advantage centred'; it also needs to be 'mission centred'.

We now understand that mission is not exclusive to any one nation or people, but is from anywhere to everywhere. Once, Western nations were responsible for taking the gospel to unreached nations around the world, but now there is no exclusive mission-force country. Today, people travel in every direction and, consequently, the monoculture mission approach is outdated. Therefore, it is vital to work together.

Leaders also need vision to discern changing paradigms. Our world is rapidly changing in cultural terms. Therefore, to reach the unchurched and to equip members for contemporary ministry, it is vital to keep up

---

[9] David Garrison, *Church Planting Movements* (Midlothian, VA: Wigtake Resources, 2004), p144.

with the transition from monocultural community to multicultural community that is occurring. As missiologist Howard Snyder looks to the future, he points out, 'We are now living under the "pressure of the future" in a way that has never been.'[10] Many authors are agreed on this. The missiologists Robinson and Smith suggest that 'dramatic change [is] required of the church'.[11] In other words, a vision for the future demands change in the present. The church at present is not likely to be the church of tomorrow. The monocultural church does not reflect the multi-ethnic missional church the future needs.

But responding to this vision demands passion.

Passion

One way in which I have cultivated a missional culture attitude is by attending a variety of Christian events, especially those which attract leaders from host culture churches. In these gatherings, one can learn about vision and missional strategy.

I have always been puzzled about the decline of the Church in the UK, when indigenous church leaders seem to have great strategies for reaching their communities. One of the reasons I have observed for this disconnect between strategy and actual results is that the host culture churches seem to lack passion for mission (or at least this is a critique I bring from my cultural perspective). It is not likely that one can engage in mission without passion, but

---

[10] Snyder, *Radical Renewal*, p187.

[11] Martin Robinson and Dwight Smith, *Invading Secular Space* (Oxford: Monarch, 2003), p107.

the fact of the matter is that in this multicultural society beset by secularism, the degree of passion required is far greater and deeper than that demonstrated at present in much ministry. Part of this has to do with the prevailing spirit of the age, in that life is easy in a consumerist context and this can lead to contentment in leaders. The apostle Paul's missionary passion for the Church was such that despite great suffering, his deep concern was for the churches he planted (2 Corinthians 11:28). Passion for the Church, and for the mission of God, is what motivates the missional leader; this alone feeds the calling to ministry and commitment to mission.

Commitment

A few years ago, in a small group discussion at a regional leadership gathering, I was asked to explain the success of my church planting. I described what I had done and how I had committed myself to the initial vision. It appeared to me that the group felt that my commitment was too much, and they joked about what I felt were small sacrifices to engage in mission for Jesus. Since then, I have become conscious of other people's approach to mission and have sadly noticed that many of the people I see conducting mission lack commitment.

I wondered whether I was doing mission the wrong way and began to cut down on the time I spent on outreach and other evangelistic activities; consequently the outcomes for my mission work also declined. Commitment matters! I have been encouraged by a leader from Mizoram in India who also shares great commitment for evangelism and church planting, as well as other leaders in some networks I engage in.

The capacity to withstand the pressures of leadership, especially in changing circumstances, is to be seen in the leader's commitment. The commitment of a leader recharges their determination. It helps the leader to ride the storm and to forge ahead, despite the odds. Commitment does not imply being blind or closed to reality. Rather, it is having the tenacity and determination to think outside the box, the resolve to find a way to accomplish the vision. Commitment is born of an informed or intelligent decision, after considering the demands on things such as time, energy and resources. Commitment often requires that sacrifices be made!

It is commonly reported by ministers that their families can suffer, as well as the churches we serve, if there are too few people engaged in ministry to meet internal needs and broader missional outreach programmes. This underlines the importance of identifying and raising up other leaders from among a church's membership.

Integrity

The leader's character and personal integrity helps to identify them as a 'leader' in the missional community. It is much harder work in the late modern context to win the trust of secular people. They no longer accept that there is one simple truth to find, but multiple possibilities relativise any discussion of one truth, such as Christians avow to be found in Christ. They are suspicious of the motives of leaders. Hence it is even more vital for a leader to have authentic character traits of integrity and honesty in the light of this prevailing cultural critique of leaders in general.

The personal qualities, character, or nature of the leader is the foundation upon which the success of leadership can be built. In their book *The Missional Leader*, the church planting thinkers Roxburgh and Romanuk suggest, 'Missional leadership is first about character and formation.'[12] Leaders' lives need to be above reproach as they model godly character to their community. Paul emphasised this in his instruction to Timothy for appointing church leaders: the 'overseer must be above reproach' (1 Timothy 3:2). Since leaders are responsible for leading the community and will be taking their people into new and challenging situations, they will need to have confidence in their credibility both as a Christian and as a leader.

Roxburgh and Romanuk, in discussing the identity and character of a leader, show the effect that the leader's life and example has on members: 'The questions people in a congregation often ask, indirectly or obviously, concern whether or not they can trust the leader.'[13] People need to trust and respect the leaders because of who they are. It is the element of 'being', a people-person of integrity rather than someone who seeks position and power in organisations. As Walter Wright says, 'Leadership is a relationship of trust. We listen to people we trust. We

---

[12] Alan Roxburgh and Fred Romanuk, *The Missional Leader* (San Francisco, CA: Jossey-Bass, 2006), p126.

[13] Roxburgh and Romanuk, *The Missional Leader*, p126.

accept the influence of a person whose character we respect.'[14]

However, every leader has both strengths and weaknesses. One weakness may be using power in the wrong way. As Lord Acton famously said, 'Power tends to corrupt, and absolute power corrupts absolutely.'[15]

There are two basic ways in which power is exercised. The good use of power entails love, humility, self-limitation, joy, vulnerability, submission, freedom. In contrast, the bad use of power involves destruction of relationships, pride and arrogance, enforcing the Law rather than the spirit of the law, lust for wealth and sex, hedonism and narcissism, spin, ends justifying means. The Old Testament requirements for choosing a king in Deuteronomy (17:14-20) warn against these areas of weakness and temptation. Paul tells Titus that a leader who is entrusted with God's work 'must be above reproach' (Titus 1:7).

Part of integrity in leadership is the willingness to act as a servant. Jesus is a good example of this. He described Himself as one who 'came not to be served but to serve' (Matthew 20:28). Therefore, in following the Master, missional leaders need to be servants. Some people want to become leaders because they desire the position and the power. Missional leaders have a different motivation. They are cautious, not wishing to push themselves forward. But

---

[14] Walter Wright, *Relational Leadership* (Milton Keynes: Paternoster Press, 2000), p15.

[15] www.phrases.org.uk/meanings/absolute-power-corrupts-absolutely.html (accessed 22nd May 2017).

at the same time they are obedient to their calling, and are willing to accept the position.

Other people have natural leadership gifts and are 'born leaders'. It is possible that born leaders will find it difficult to act in humility as servant leaders. However, training can help overcome this problem. Challenges in ministry can also shape the character of leaders, and holding them accountable in these challenges helps qualify them for leadership – though not all born leaders will respond well to challenges that call for sacrifice.

In practice, the servant leader will have care for the interests of those they lead. Their main satisfaction will be in others' growth and development. Such leaders will not mind moving chairs or getting their hands dirty. In addition, reflective practice encourages missional leaders to be accountable and to be willing to listen to and respect other peoples' views.

The leader is a servant but is expected to be decisive, willing to take responsibility and to get things done. Inherently, the leader is a risk-taker, but only after considering the various factors involved. They then accept accountability if things go wrong. Only in this way will the leader be trusted by the people. This means being fully in touch with them so that decisions made are also owned by them.

The leader needs to be open, transparent and real, and this calls for vulnerability. Such leaders will be vulnerable to being hurt by criticism, questioning, opposition and disloyalty. People are likely to follow someone who is real and who is the same whatever the situation, who does not pretend to be anything other than they are. In some cultures this is more difficult to do than in others. Some African leaders are considered to be the 'Man of God', or the prophetic authoritative voice of the Church, and it is hard to exercise this level of transparency when viewed like this.

The apostle Paul is a good role model for any aspiring missional leader. He did not hide his weaknesses from others. To the Corinthian church, he often mentioned his weaknesses and said, 'To the weak I became weak, that I might win the weak' (1 Corinthians 9:22). Revealing weakness to others shows the leader's need of support and prayer, but they also need to lean on God's power to help overcome such weaknesses. The Lord assured Paul, 'My grace is sufficient for you, for my power is made perfect in weakness' (2 Corinthians 12:9).

The leader has to cope with criticism, but some criticism can be positive, when it comes from those who want to see progress. It is good for any leader to have trusted members who can give constructive criticism. Their views should be respected, examined and used appropriately. Negative criticism sometimes arises when there is disagreement, with the leader coming from a genuine difference of perspective, but it may also come from personal rivalry. This can be dealt with in various ways, but always with firmness and grace.

The leader should first deal with critics privately, and if the matter is not resolved, then it should be brought out into the open. It is important, however, that the multi-ethnic leader bears in mind that the context in which they have been called into leadership will be subjected to sometimes contradictory criticism, so the leader should not allow themselves to be defined or personally driven by criticism. In these circumstances it is necessary to be patient and to take time to examine the reasons behind the opposition. Culturally intelligent leaders understand that various cultural and ethnic values influence the way people relate to them. Personal emotions such as anger ought to be avoided.

To summarise this chapter, the diagram below illustrates the four catalytic qualities of the multi-ethnic missional leader:

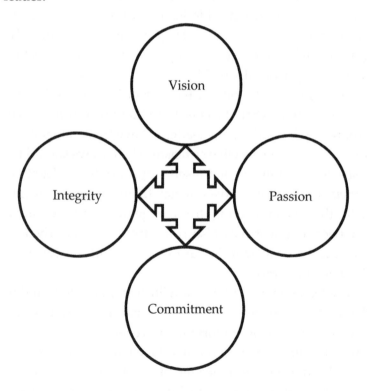

Reflection

I invite you to engage in some reflections that may help you to reflect on the qualities of good leadership.

- *Rank the four catalytic qualities given in the diagram in order of importance, from your perspective.*

- *Which of these are innate or 'inborn' and which can be worked on?*

- *Identify which qualities you need to work at, and outline a plan to achieve this.*

Chapter Three

Primary Skills of Culturally Intelligent Leadership

The type of leader needed in a multi-ethnic missional community is one who is able to understand the complex and sometimes contradictory elements of such multicultural groups. Unique and vital skills include cultural literacy, relational intelligence, emotional intelligence, creative intelligence, team formation and conflict resolution. This chapter discusses these skills.

Cultural literacy

At present, many churches that aspire to develop multi-ethnic congregations fail. This failure can come because of real and practical difficulties that are not easily dealt with if there is a lack of experience and cultural understanding that causes difficulties in communication. Even making a start towards forming multi-ethnic churches often fails because of a fear of having to deal with unfamiliar cultures. The need to establish multi-ethnic communities has been widely recognised; nevertheless, much groundwork needs to be done to understand and accept other cultures before attempting to launch multi-ethnic missional communities.

To form a new multi-ethnic church, leaders need to possess cultural literacy, without which it would be difficult to bring about a shared sense of what it means to be missional.

In their recent book, my colleagues Andy Hardy and Dan Yarnell, who teach theology and mission, discuss in detail the importance of what the leadership thinker David Livermore calls 'cultural intelligence'. They highlight the importance of multi-ethnic leaders using cultural intelligence skills. A cultural quotient (CQ), or cultural intelligence, is the ability to effectively understand and relate to another culture different to one's own. It includes the ability to ask the right questions that will get to the heart of the different aspects of another culture. These cultural questions include those that relate to understanding the norms associated with the way those within a cultural group relate to each other, and their deep values. It also includes a questioning of their world view. The culturally intelligent leader will seek to understand how those from other cultures interpret the world, their place in it and their goals.

It is impossible to understand a culture different to our own unless we become aware of what their use of language means, as it comes from their cultural background. If we do not understand what is meant by simple things, such as the way family life is valued, then we might find ourselves causing offence because we do not show the proper cultural respect towards family members with whom we seek to interact. In a patriarchal family culture, it can be considered an offence to seek to relate to family members without first greeting the father and obtaining his blessing.

Hence there is much to be learned when we seek to interact on a cross-cultural level.

In brief, Livermore articulates a four-step process that leaders who possess good cultural intelligence will exercise. These are:

Step 1 – CQ drive

The leader who wants to develop the ability to work with other leaders cross-culturally needs to have high motivation, interest, confidence and drive to adapt their thinking and behaviours. Livermore offers a sharp profile of such a leader:

> Leaders with high CQ drive are motivated to learn and adapt to new diverse cultural settings. Their confidence in their adaptive abilities is likely to influence the way they perform in multicultural situations.[16]

Arguably, a lack of motivation to get to know another culture will lead to little effort. Leaders who are effective in intercultural missional ministry will need to be highly motivated to do the groundwork that is necessary in order to really get to know the cultural group they want to work among.

In multi-ethnic churches, missional leaders will need to get to know each other's cultures, as well as have the drive to get to know the cultures of the broader church membership. Anything less will inevitably lead to

---

[16] Livermore paraphrased by Hardy and Yarnell, *Forming Multicultural Partnerships*, pp174-175.

increased misunderstandings, if it is assumed that we can treat one another in the same manner in each cultural context.

Step 2 – CQ knowledge

This simply has to do with a leader's ability to understand the issues and differences that exist between their culture and the culture they want to work with. Livermore offers this profile of a leader who is developing CQ knowledge:

> Leaders high in CQ knowledge have rich, well-organized understanding of culture and how it affects the way people think and behave. They possess a repertoire of knowledge in knowing how cultures are alike and different. They understand how culture shapes behavior.[17]

This next step demonstrates where the real hard work is to be located. Having a rich understanding of another culture takes time to obtain. It means giving hospitality and receiving it. It means a heavy investment in time where the leaders make themselves available to build relationships with other leaders, their families and the families of those leaders' own culture. Moreover, it is important for leaders to model genuine interest in understanding others if they wish others to learn from their approaches and use these approaches themselves. In other words, members from different cultural backgrounds in multi-ethnic churches will hopefully start

---

[17] Hardy and Yarnell, *Forming Multicultural Partnerships*, p177.

to learn about each other's cultures in similar ways, using approaches modelled to them by their leaders.

Step 3 – CQ strategy

This step relates to how we make sense of our knowledge of cross-cultural differences, which will help us to formulate effective strategies to be able to work with a new group. Livermore offers the following profile of a leader who is developing CQ strategy:

> Leaders with high CQ strategy develop ways to use cultural understanding to develop a plan for new cross-cultural situations. These leaders are better able to monitor, analyze, and adjust their behaviors in different cultural settings. They are conscious of what they need to know about unfamiliar culture.[18]

As much as anything else here, Livermore raises the vital strategic question of the leader's posture. In other words, leaders with high CQ will seek to ask themselves questions about the impact of their behaviours on the people from other cultural backgrounds in their churches. This requires the posture of what is termed a strategic mindset. The leader with a high CQ will be a strategist at the level of knowing their impact on others, as well as the impact of different cultural groups in the church on each other. The leadership team will need to monitor carefully developments in the relationships among members of differing cultures in order to help them understand each

---

[18] Hardy and Yarnell, *Forming Multicultural Partnerships*, p182.

other better, as well as being able to relate to each other better. This is vital if conflicts are to be resolved and misunderstandings addressed.

Step 4 – CQ action

The action phase of any leadership planning concerns the hoped-for outcomes from interaction with a target group. In the case of CQ action, it is necessary to use appropriate verbal and non-verbal actions so that we can interact cross-culturally. Livermore offers this profile of a leader who is developing CQ action abilities:

> Leaders with high CQ action can draw on the other three dimensions of CQ to translate their enhanced motivation, understanding, and planning into action. They possess a broad repertoire of behaviors, which they can use depending on the context.[19]

Making such cultural connections takes energy and time as the leader creates ways of communicating with those outside the church and encourages the members to do the same. What is important for a culturally intelligent leader to recognise is that seeking to contextualise Christian beliefs for other cultures must not be done at the expense of compromising the Christian message.

Culture encodes every person's perspectives, so we cannot ignore how people of different cultures might understand things differently when communicating interculturally. This means that culturally intelligent

---

[19] Hardy and Yarnell, *Forming Multicultural Partnerships*, p184.

leaders need to develop the capacity to check that what they think they are communicating is actually being interpreted as they expect by those with whom they communicate from another culture. This takes time, and it will not be immediately obvious how cultural differences cause us to interpret what is communicated. For example, people from an honour–shame culture find it hard to lose face if they are perceived to have failed in some way. Many Westerners take it to be vital that each individual takes responsibility for their strengths and weaknesses, whereas in an honour–shame culture it is taken for granted that a person be given a way to save face without being held to account by a public acknowledgement of a weakness. This is one example of how cross-cultural conflict can occur if a Westerner insists on forcing an issue where public responsibility is demanded of someone from such a culture.

Cultural intelligence requires understanding of how cultural matters like honour–shame work, and then learning to think how to help someone address an issue so that required adjustments can be made without causing conflict. Reading popular books in the field of cultural anthropology can help a leader to develop understanding and to increase their cultural intelligence. Another approach might be to obtain a mentor who understands the particular culture the leader is seeking to deepen knowledge of.

Churches are being planted in many different ways relevant to the cultures around them. The church-planting thinker David Beer discusses some well-known new church models. For instance, the Seeker Movement focuses on creative ways of reaching outsiders with the gospel and has inspired manifestations such as café-style or 'Menu' church, or meeting in Starbucks, or pub churches, or where people work. Such meetings may not be on Sundays. The cell church movement is described as a church that meets primarily in small groups and has been particularly effective in Anglican churches and new church plants. There are several expressions of cell church, including home churches. The Emerging Churches came out of the Generation X churches of the 1980s linked to postmodernity, and exist largely as youth congregations within established churches or as independent churches using contemporary music and technology.[20] We might add to these the practitioners of 'simple church' and the various neo-monastic church movements.

There are many options, but the leader needs to consider which model is best suited to a given situation or vision. They may, for example, be in a traditional church, and not want to carry traditional church practices into a new church situation. In such a case, care must be taken to ensure that team members do not carry their old traditions into the new church and thus make it a clone.

At the same time, the leader needs to consider how to bring change gradually without losing people. This may mean mixing new practices with the old in some form of contextualisation.

---

[20] David Beer, *Releasing Your Church to Grow* (Eastbourne: Kingsway, 2004), pp18-27.

Relational intelligence

The relational leader is someone who not only has ideas, but can also communicate their vision to others. Tom Marshall comments, 'Leaders must not only conceptualize the goals, they must articulate them and communicate them to other people.'[21]

The ability to communicate can be enhanced by ensuring some basic approaches to communication. Crucially, communication is a two-way process. People should not be seen as a means to an end, but as of worth in their own right – only then will our communication with them become effective. The leader and the people for whom the leader is responsible are engaged in a mutual relationship. Both are involved in sending and receiving communication with each other.

In a multi-ethnic community, clarity in communication is important. Such clarity helps elevate the quality of relationship building, which is a complex process considering the plurality and diversity of language and symbolism contributed by the multicultural setting. This means the leader is operating in a complex environment, and this calls for honesty in the communication process.

When the leader exercises honest communication, trust is built up within the missional community. Communication skills are related to cultural literacy in the sense that 'I say A, you hear Z', and there is the possibility of confusion, and yet the missional leader can also turn this

---

[21] Tom Marshall, *Understanding Leadership* (Chichester: Sovereign World, 1991), p130.

potential problem into an opportunity for missional engagement. For example, if a person from a highly hospitable culture, as many African cultures can be, takes offence because an offer of hospitality has not been accepted, then the opportunity would be to invest in showing hospitality to an offended party in a special way that makes them feel an honoured guest. The experience could become an opportunity for missional engagement in which a relationship or friendship is forged that could lead to winning a sister or brother for Christ.

Jesus is a good example of someone who communicated relationally. He cared for people, met with them, visited their homes and spoke to their felt needs. In the same vein, the missional leader should break or overcome excessive individualism by developing relationships in order to create an atmosphere for engagement with the community. Roxburgh and Romanuk suggest that one task of leaders is to 'cultivate an environment in which the boundary-breaking spirit constantly calls forth new ways of being God's community'.[22] This is in line with the view mentioned earlier, that leaders are risk-takers.

Relationships are dynamic ties, constantly changing, and so relational intelligence equips the leader with the necessary understanding and framework to access new ways of being missional and being God's people. Meeting members personally can achieve this formation of God's community, as well as the use of modern technologies such as the internet, telephone, texts, email and social media.

---

[22] Roxburgh and Romanuk, *The Missional Leader*, p124.

One of the attractions of a newly planted church will be the fact that it is relational, thus outsiders, who often lack meaningful relationships, will be drawn in. Often church plants begin small and have a higher than average relational quotient and openness to outsiders than established churches.

Andy Hardy comments in his most recent book, *Pictures of God: Shaping Missional Church Life,* that every community bases its relationships on how it views God and His relationship with His people. He speaks of how Christian communities that rely on relationships based on *agape* love need to take their understanding of how to love each other from the way God has exhibited His unconditional love to humanity. He suggests that relational intelligence is based on the degree of intimacy that exists between God and believers and between each person in the church. If God is pictured to be a relational, loving Father Who can be approached with confidence and without fear of condemnation, then such a vision will motivate God's multi-ethnic people to treat each other with hospitality, grace, forgiveness and unconditional positive regard. Hardy offers eleven ways that a multi-ethnic missional leader can be enabled to understand how to help people relate to each other better. These are:

1.   Discover the founding story of your Christian community. Understanding what drew people together when a community was founded helps reveal what makes them tick, and what brought them together. This mirrors the dynamic used by marriage counsellors who ask a couple whose

marriage is in trouble what first brought them together. Reconnecting with the romance, attraction and love ignites and fuels relationships.

2. Actively listen to the stories of the people in your community. Active listening requires that you pay careful attention to people's stories that tell you who they are, what they struggle with and what they hope for. Listen carefully for emotions and feelings as they reveal what makes them happy, sad, excited, etc. In other words, it is necessary to see things from their perspective and hence come to appreciate them for who they are. This also means they can come to understand you better in similar ways.

3. What does the locality you meet in, and its environment, say about your community's picture of God? The places where people like to meet reveal a lot about the kinds of things they like to do together. For example, a church that is set up like a café, with tables and chairs for people to sit at while meeting to worship or pray, might suggest a high value of hospitality, sharing a coffee and having a chat with friends.

4. What voluntary ministries are people involved in outside the church, or within it? It is quite common for Christians to volunteer some free time to do things that fit their gifting and interests. What kinds of things do people value in your community? What do the things they do tell you about the kinds of

relationships they have with the people they work with?

5.   How do outsiders see God reflected in your community? The missiologist Lesslie Newbigin once said that the local church is the hermeneutic of the gospel. What he meant by this was that as people look at how Christians behave they should be able to see the God of love, reconciliation and relationship shining out of their lives. You can learn much from how others see your Christian community, as it will tell you how much love, welcome and generosity of friendship they experience from its people.

6.   How do members see Jesus reflected in each other and in the Christian community? Scripture tells us that we can see the light of the knowledge of the glory of God shining in the face of Jesus who shines in our hearts by His Holy Spirit. There is much to be learned by looking for Jesus in others as He is the key to all reconciliation and friendships. Friendships are the glue of relationships and they need to be the goal for multi-ethnic leaders in their missional communities.

7.   What is God's purpose for your community? People need purpose. Good relationships are based on commonly shared goals and purposes, among other things. What is the goal of your community's life and ministry, if not a longing for the final establishment of God's kingdom of peace? A Christian community displaying genuine friendships among its people

will find many opportunities for deep spiritual relationships. At the heart of God's goal for creation is that we become the friends of God and one another.

8. What is your community's vision and mission statement? What does this have to do with relationships? Scripture says the people perish for the lack of vision (Proverbs 29:18, KJV). At the heart of a vision statement is that which captures the dreams of a missional community. Good vision statements must not be artificial – they capture our passion for the future with God. Shared dreams are the stuff of strong relationships.

9. Who are the people joining your community and what attracted them to your community? People of course seek to join churches for many reasons, but what is often heard is that a new attendee was attracted because of the care, support and love offered to them by people in the community. This means we can learn much about what is valued by the people who come to join with us.

10. What are the most common things people in our Christian community say that express how they identify with their community? Every congregation will have some common sayings that are often heard on the lips of members. What do you hear them say? For example, someone might say, 'This is a cold place sometimes.' Do they mean it is literally cold or feels cold emotionally?

11. What do your enemies say about your community? This is much harder, but people who have left churches often hold grudges or resentments against the church. It can be informative to listen to what our enemies say about us, as often there can be uncomfortable relational revelations that are much closer to the truth than we would like to admit. In some churches, disenfranchised former members are approached in what is termed 'reclamation ministry', to see whether healing can be brought and relationships restored. This will call for forgiveness and letting go of the past if new friendships are to be forged.[23]

How does all of this relate to the kind of relational intelligence we need to develop in order to build the relational capital of our missional churches? Most importantly, it centres on a leadership team seeking to take time to look at their multi-ethnic missional communities through a number of lenses, such as the ones suggested by Hardy, in order to become more relationally informed about themselves and more relationally intelligent. The goal is for your missional community to be founded on the grace and love of Christ, the one we are told we can call 'friend', and Who calls all of us to love each other as much as we love God and ourselves.

---

[23] Andrew R Hardy, *Pictures of God* (Watford: Instant Apostle, 2016), pp236-242.

Emotional intelligence

Working with people tends to involve having to deal with various emotions. Emotional intelligence is a necessary skill in a multi-ethnic community, because leaders often have to deal with negative emotions which result from perceived insensitivity from those of a different cultural background. It is important to positively deal with the causes of the feelings of hurt rather than overreacting in panic, which can cause the parties concerned to feel that an issue is bigger and harder to resolve than it really is.

Emotional intelligence demands a level of nuanced understanding on the part of the missional leader. For example, in my experience, the expression of grief in some cultures does not necessarily translate into loud wailing or crying. Emotional intelligence considers the fact that a lack or absence of tears does not mean that the person concerned is not experiencing pain or loss. Taking this further, it might be that for the individual and the community they belong to, shedding tears is not considered appropriate. Emotional intelligence requires the leader to correctly interpret the underlying meaning behind whatever verbal communication is being offered.

It is important to recognise that there can be additional sources of hidden hurt behind much communication people have with their leaders and each other in multi-ethnic missional communities. One area of hidden hurt might come from power abuse, where one ethnic group may hold a cultural memory of feeling oppressed by another group. For example, in some Afro-Caribbean churches, there can be long-held memories regarding slavery and the perceived pain of a people downtrodden and treated as less than human. Such memories can sometimes remain from an earlier period in life when family stories of racial hatred from one group towards another was a common theme talked of by parents. These 'frozen' emotions can be unlocked in multi-ethnic churches when someone from one group does something to hurt the feelings of someone from another group. Suddenly old memories and prejudices that have been deeply felt as part of a family's history can come rushing to the surface. What is called for in this case is a healing process of past hurts and memories to take place.

In relation to this experience, a classic book written by the popular pastoral counsellor David Seamands, *Healing for Damaged Emotions*, is well worth reading. Seamands talks of how the restoring love of Christ can bring about peace and healing to old wounds. In another book by the same author, *Healing of Memories*, he sets out the need to bring into conscious life some of the memories that cause us to still feel grieved and wounded. In multi-ethnic churches, historical memories of power abuse, racial hatred and the association of present-day people whose ancestors abused a people group now worshipping in the same church can call for a special ministry where memories are brought to the Lord for healing. This calls for emotional intelligence, and the multi-ethnic leadership team will need to consider how to consult those with expertise in these areas to help reconciliation to take place through the healing of damaged emotions which live on in historically based memories.

Moreover, racial bullying can be found not just outside churches but also inside them, especially in multi-ethnic churches. It is of fundamental importance for leaders to deal with anything that is perceived to be any form of racial bullying. And this is where great sensitivity is required, because what might seem like a rather minor instance of a bad joke poorly made must not be minimised. For example, a joke about a person's skin colour, facial features, accent or clothes may be made innocently, but could lead to a breakdown in inter-personal relationships in the multi-ethnic community. What can help in these situations are some basic ground rules that everyone agrees to – for example, not to make personal jokes about others, even if they are taken well. The high priority in these cases is to assure that sensitivity to others' feelings is protected.

Overall, emotional intelligence in cross-cultural communication is not intuitive for most people. If we have not spent time around people of other cultures, then we simply may not have developed the capacity and sensitivity to have empathy with them, to see things from their perspective. We cannot know what it would feel like to feel shamed in a Chinese church, for example, because we may not have ever experienced what it feels like to live in a culture where honour and shame are big deals, with deep emotions attached to them.

Creative intelligence

In a postmodern and increasingly secular society, the missional leader will need to exercise creative intelligence in terms of developing skills to find effective ways of reaching the community with the message of the gospel. David Beer suggests:

> Against the background of an overall decline in church attendance, there are new and innovative examples of new or changing churches in all kinds of social and cultural settings.[24]

The proliferation of new ways of communicating has led to the establishment of new ways of being community. Facebook or Twitter-based communities are being formed by some creative missional leaders to meet particular needs. These are communities in the sense that the people who participate begin to strongly identify with each other via issues of common interest. These communities are not defined by geography, culture, social status or any other artificial or biological barrier. In some cases, these online or cyber communities are not even dictated by a specific religious or denominational affiliation. The creative missional leader not only understands the new ways of being community, but also ensures through the resources available to the leadership that creative and imaginative responses are used to engage with the new ways of being community.

Creativity will affect the ways in which communication is achieved. Whether it is through the effective use of new media or technology, creativity will also affect the responses of leaders to issues faced by communities. An

---

[24] Beer, *Releasing Your Church to Grow*, p18.

Ethiopian singer, Kefa Mideksa, has at the time of writing more than 29,700 followers and 4,869 friends on his Facebook page. Such a community is statistically in sharp contrast to some churches with a typical average membership of fifty people. This is not to say big is beautiful and small is to be looked down on. Rather, the point I am making is that different kinds of communities, be they cyber in nature like Facebook, or a small church, need to value those they communicate with. Obviously the larger the numbers the less intimate the communication, but in today's world communication and being linked in with others, like pop stars or personally favoured role models, is important. One pastor, Reverend Robin Brookes of Famagusta in Cyprus, is known to keep in touch with his members through Facebook.

The potential for missional engagement online is vast, as evidenced by the way Twitter and Facebook have been used to raise awareness, to organise protests or to generate support for or campaign on a given matter. Creativity recognises and takes advantage of what God is doing and rides with it, whether in a small church or on social media. Creativity is needed to refresh, revive and motivate multi-ethnic missional communities.

Team formation

The Bible shows that the idea of teams has been a common and acceptable practice for a long time. The Trinity as *missio communitatis*, the community of the Godhead – God the Father, God the Son and God the Holy Spirit – is an example of the perfect, prime team. Jesus Himself formed

His first team of twelve apostles, and the early Church apostles followed His example by establishing teams wherever they planted new churches. Acts 2 leaves us in no doubt that the early converts to Christianity, although Jews, came to Jerusalem from around the Empire at Pentecost, and they were almost certainly influenced by a variety of ethnic and cultural backgrounds.

The book of Acts raises the importance of cross-cultural, or should we say intercultural, teams. People respond well to people from their own culture, and at first new converts are best discipled by people who understand them well. An intercultural team can meet this need.

The leadership writer Andy Stanley points out, 'Leadership is not always about getting things done "right." Leadership is about getting things done through people.' [25] This shifts attention from the leader as an individual to the leader as a collective, leadership not as one person but leadership as a team. Multi-ethnic teams make for a special kind of collective that can facilitate the negotiation of understanding between different subgroups in a multicultural missional church context. Sometimes this requires courage on the part of the church leader. For example, in building a team, the mature leader is willing to recruit others with greater abilities than they might have, without fear of being overshadowed. That might mean recruiting those with great potential without the fear that the fostering of this potential will lead to the original or recruiting leader becoming redundant. In truth, this might indeed happen. The positive way to view this is that the

[25] Stanley, *Next Generation Leader*, p27.

original leaders have worked themselves out of a job and are now free to begin other new projects. Such a view recognises that the kingdom of God is full of opportunities and that God is calling many people to accomplish the innumerable tasks demanded in mission. The missional leader therefore realises what is needed, relies on God in everything, and releases other leaders in teamwork.

The leader who is able to delegate builds a team within which all the necessary skills are represented. This team brings together the skills, experience and insight of the members for their common goal. Team leadership thinkers Katzenbach and Smith have said:

> Teams should be the basic unit of performance for most organizations ... in any situations requiring the real-time combination of multiple skills, experiences, and judgements; a team inevitably gets better results than a collection of individuals.[26]

Effective teams harness synergy; they bring together people with different skills and experience whose combined output is more than that of the individuals working separately. As teams establish mutual trust and confidence and a sense of respect and accountability, change and growth can take place.

Good teams also bring together people with technical expertise, problem-solving and decision-making abilities, and interpersonal skills. The mix and blend of members

---

[26] Jon R Katzenbach and Douglas K Smith, *The Wisdom of Teams* (London: McKinsey & Company, 2003), p15.

should include a range of functions such as a 'Catalyst' (the visionary, the one with ideas and creativity, the one who sets goals and direction), an 'Organiser' (the one who converts vision into reality, who sees how ideas and objectives can be realised, who brings order) and a 'Maintainer' (the one who keeps the show on the road, who manages the project and ensures that it is completed).[27]

The team needs to be small enough for its members to communicate and meet easily, to have an agreed purpose that excites the members, and to share a sense of mutual accountability. There are genuine anxieties and concerns facing people when they join a team. There are risks, which include personality conflicts, and fear of the accountability that is necessary. It takes time and energy on the part of the leader to build trust and a sense of interdependence within the team. When it works well, the team provides the best system for the delivery of performance.

Conflict resolution

In any situation where the Church is advancing, there will be opposition. Unfortunately, conflict can also arise within the missional team. Although this can be destructive, it can also help the team to grow. A strong, solid team will experience conflict which will lead to the acquisition of the virtues of trust and interdependence.

Teams bring together people from different backgrounds and experiences, and with different ideas and

---

[27] See the work of Meredith Belbin for a fuller explanation of these terms.

expectations. It is good for them to talk through their differences, as 'Iron sharpens iron' (Proverbs 27:17). Sometimes, when team members cannot agree, conflict will arise which is potentially damaging and, if not handled with sensitivity and tact, might lead to wounding, hurt, misunderstanding and frustration, causing the team to fail to achieve its mission.

The constituency and composition of the multi-ethnic community will inherently harbour disagreement. Therefore, it is incumbent upon the leader to manage this conflict. The roots of conflict lie in pride and obstinacy, and strongly cherished opinions. This is particularly likely in missional situations with people who are confident of their leadership gifting.

Conflict was apparent even in the early Church initially, in the dispute about the treatment of widows in Acts 6, and later in the sharp division between Paul and Barnabas over John Mark (Acts 15:36-41). Today, similar conflicts can arise, brought on by criticism of the leader and the leadership team, by complaints of neglect by groups that believe themselves to have been marginalised, by complaints that strongly held views have been ignored or not properly listened to, and by complaints that vocal and strongly opinionated individuals dominate.

Conflict centred on music, theology or churchmanship can also arise between traditionalists and modernists. Additional conflict can be caused by troublemakers with their own agendas creating divisions and factions, gossip and betrayal of trust. In the multi-ethnic community, the propensity for conflict is high because it embraces diversity and therefore difference. It is like sitting on a time bomb in the sense that it is committed to respecting difference and yet it is true also that difference, say in understanding mission, in matters of doctrine, in values, traditions, customs and other characteristics of the members, can lead to serious and sometimes negative results. Each constituent sector of the community will articulate a need that might be different from the needs of the other members. Conflict management in these cases involves the ability to read the situation beforehand and to effect measures to deal with any potential conflict. Conflicts that are not quickly resolved can produce paralysis in the team's progress towards achieving its objectives. Signs of this paralysis include loss of energy and enthusiasm, difficulty in coming to agreements and making decisions, a loss of purpose, cynicism and mistrust, gossip, and personal attacks behind people's backs.

Sometimes, missional leaders may themselves be the cause of conflict. As the spiritual contemplative Thomas à Kempis stated, 'We cannot trust ourselves too much because grace and understanding are often lacking in us.'[28] In this case, the leader should, firstly, listen to other team members; secondly, not reply sharply to negative ideas; and, thirdly, take time to think how to deal with the situation. In addition, the leaders need to consult their own mentors as soon as problems arise. If they do not solve these problems as soon as possible, it is very likely that the vision will fail.

It is possible for conflicts to arise between churches in a district, especially where other local churches do not share

[28] Thomas à Kempis, *The Imitation of Christ* (Orlando, FL: Bridge-Logos, 1999), p92.

a vision for mission. As the causes of conflict differ from area to area and time to time, leaders who seek to plant new churches need to seek to form alliances and common understanding with other local church leaders in order to quiet their fears that actually the church planter, as a newcomer, is seeking to undermine their ministry in an area. We don't do mission because we like a community we want to reach, but because God loves all nations and has salvific purposes for them.

If there are unreached people groups in a region, which existing churches are not reaching, then ways may be sought to establish the case for a new church plant. This is at the heart of the establishment of multi-ethnic missional communities as well. Since leaders and their members are sent by God to play this role on the earth, they always need to encourage their own congregation to live in peace with each other, and they need to engage in effective strategies for living with other faith communities in other churches and outside the Church, as that is also a way of demonstrating the gospel. If a church planter seeks to plant a church in an area that has more than one unreached people group, then other local church leaders may be asked to offer support to the planter and their team, even if it be prayer support for the task at hand.

Conflicts can take up much energy and time to resolve, since dealing with issues of trust and interdependence requires hard work and patience. They therefore need to be confronted early. Disagreements must not be allowed to grow into a breakdown of relationships. Leaders need the skills to resolve conflict by bringing opposing parties together to encourage mutual respect and love. It is imperative to listen to all the parties involved and to encourage them to discuss their differences with each other. Keeping the goals and purpose before the team will help to build commitment and confidence, thus securing the desired outcome.

Having noted the above, the causes of conflict can be complex to understand and far from easy to resolve if the conflict has continued for a long period of time. Hence a high priority in a multi-ethnic church is the speedy resolution of conflict before people become entrenched in positions and therefore less willing to dialogue to bring about a resolution to the conflict. Some of the main causes of conflict in multi-ethnic churches arise primarily from misinterpretation of the behaviours of people, which may appear to be aimed at showing offence, when in fact they may simply be a normal way that people relate to each other. An example might be that in a Western culture, being exact about time-keeping is a sign of respect to the host, whereas in another culture, time is measured in a much more relaxed manner where people expect lateness, and actually the lateness is just part of a more relaxed outlook on the priorities of life.

The word 'conflict' comes from the Latin *Flege*, which means to strike together. The striking together of two pieces of flint causes sparks. When people strike together because of cultural misunderstanding, relational and emotional sparks are caused. Conflict implies difference between people, which leads to tension. This tension can cause arguments and a rupture in a relationship.

It is important to address conflicts when they cause disruption and disagreement. In the Church, unity is a high priority and forgiveness is vital. However, it is hard to forgive someone if the cause of the offence and the conflict is not resolved. Obstacles may form between people, which can lead to inflexibility and division into camps, where one party insists they are absolutely right while those in the other party insist the same. Moreover, it can also lead to competition between two people or groups who then seek to get things done their way, to the annoyance and neglect of the other. We are talking, in other words, about the formation of people who view the other/s as in some sense enemies, or if not enemies, to be untrustworthy and thus to be avoided.

Escalation can be another danger of cross-cultural misunderstandings that lead to conflict. For example, if one group or person is angry with another, it can lead to greater hostility, which in the end means that a rift will happen in a fellowship or between people. Anger is a demanding emotion. It demands to have things its way. If it becomes deeply held and there is no resolution, it can also lead to bitterness and resentment, which are a far worse kind of conflict. Hence it is important that people can learn how to say what they feel without attacking others, that they are able to communicate gently and firmly what their anger makes them want to demand.

This is where some basic insights from counselling can help in terms of conflict resolution between family members or groups. Counsellors seek to encourage people in conflict to express their emotions in less threatening or potentially offensive ways. It can therefore make all the difference in the world for the missional leader as a conflict counsellor to act as a referee between two parties who seem to be in conflict. It will be important to establish some ground rules. One of those is to seek agreement if possible that a key goal of the Christian life is forgiveness and grace. In order to reach that goal, the referee can encourage each party in a conflict to express their anger, grief or frustration using 'I' messages, rather than 'you' messages. So, for example, instead of someone saying to the person they are in conflict with, 'It is your fault that you caused offence to my wife when you hugged her when she arrived at the prayer meeting,' the 'you' message could become an 'I' message: 'I feel that it was inappropriate for you to hug my wife, as in our culture men do not treat other men's wives like this.' This takes the accusation out of the 'you' message, and instead the feeling of the offended party is expressed in a manner which can help the one who has caused the offence to understand the real issue and emotions that the behaviour has elicited.

It is impossible in a chapter of this length to go into a full discussion of conflict resolution – this would require a book in its own right. However, one final thing to say about conflict resolution is that one very common phenomenon of conflict when it begins is that people declare their positions. Even in non-conflict situations, we may all have our particular views on what proper preaching should be, or which styles of music should be used in worship, or whether we should share a common cup for the Eucharist or separate small glasses. If we hold these positions strongly, then we may feel offended if, for example, the preacher from another cultural background does not preach as loudly and as passionately as our culture considers appropriate.

One can imagine that preaching styles and worship styles would be causes of discomfort and conflict in multi-ethnic churches. Indeed, they are. So how can we negotiate a change in the perception of what are at first strongly held positions that people seek to defend and fight for in a conflict situation, towards creating understanding of the underlying vested interests behind those positions? A Baptist Union resource that deals with conflict makes a point that will prove helpful:

> How then, do we move from positions to interests?
>
> Imagine an orange. Two people want it and they want it now. There is only one orange. What is to happen? Explore the options, e.g.:
>
> Cut it in half (compromise)
>
> Toss a coin (chance)
>
> Buy another one (expanded resources)
>
> But we could ask: What do both want the orange for?
>
> One response might be: 'I need the rind to make a cake.' The other is: 'I need the inside to extract the juice.'
>
> Here both can have what they each want. They have moved from positions to interests. This is a win/win outcome rather than a win/lose one.[29]

---

[29] V O'Brien and E Whalley, *Journeying Through Conflict: Part of Life* (Didcot: Baptist Union of Great Britain, 2010), p11.

Once people are able to express the real interests behind their stated positions, it is possible to deal with the true issues at stake.

Conflict management is part of the job of the leader, but the leader needs to be mindful of potential consequences for the community. Resolving conflict requires an understanding of the causes or sources of conflict, such as vision mismatch, miscommunication, expert knowledge, change, fear, jealousy and hurt.

How can change happen? A call for creative solutions:

1. Are there churches in your network that are struggling with issues of conflict? How are they dealing with it? Is their way of managing and dealing with it effective?

2. How can leaders like this be prevented from taking on positions of influence from the start?

3. How can training in your network address and profile the right kinds of leaders to lead congregations?

Summary of skills

The following diagram presents a summary of the primary skills of culturally intelligent missional leadership:

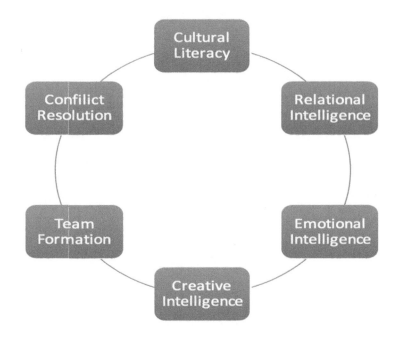

Reflection

I invite you once more to engage in some reflections on missional leadership skills.

- *Multi-ethnic missional leadership is a complex endeavour. How can the primary skills highlighted in this chapter be brought together to help form a multicultural missional community?*

- *Outline reasons why multi-ethnic missional community is necessary. Make a list of the advantages and the barriers to achieving this.*

- *Draw up a plan for fostering multicultural mission initiatives in your own locality. Who are the people most likely to relate to such an initiative?*

Part Two

Moving from Monocultural Maintenance to Multi-ethnic Missional Communities: The Kairos time!

Chapter Four

Current Missional Communities: Host Monocultural Missional Communities and Immigrant Missional Communities

In the first chapter, the case was made that some current host culture churches are made up of multi-ethnic peoples but they do not operate as multicultural churches, in the sense that they pursue a Western style of worship rather than celebrating their cultural diversity in the way they operate. I am not arguing that worshipping in a Western style is mistaken; indeed, it can enhance the contextual engagement of such churches with people in their neighbourhood. What I believe is most important, however, is for those in the leadership to come from more than one ethnic, cultural background.

There are important reasons for having a mixed leadership of this type, as it can provide a positive message that a multinational church embraces diversity. It may also be claimed that it will provide a welcoming message to those from different backgrounds that they are valued for who they are in terms of their cultural heritage. First-generation migrant peoples who have moved to the West need environments where their children, who are becoming Westernised in a way their parents are not, may benefit from a diverse mixture of intercultural opportunities to meet young people from more than just their parents' culture.

MH is a third-culture child (TCC)[30] and his father, HK, is a reverse missionary and leader of a monocultural church. However, this church no longer appeals to MH, although he still attends HK's church to be with his father and to meet other TCCs who are his friends. He is a typical representative of his generation. The state of TCCs in many missional communities is still problematic, in that although the emergence of a third-culture generation is relatively new as opposed to the parent or host culture, it does not result in immediate patterns of discipleship nor a strategy to deal with it. TCCs spend a lot of energy forging a new identity during adolescence as they bridge different cultures, and this can make it hard for them to fully integrate a Christian identity into what is an emergent identity suited to a third-culture position. It may, in other words, take longer to disciple a TCC owing to profound identity questions. If we are to address the disconnection with TCCs, the old cultures must be prepared to accommodate to the new culture.

TCCs in a first-culture home often find themselves having to deal with distinctive challenges or tensions arising between their home setting and the wider host culture in which they are growing up. The interface between parents from a first culture and their third-culture

---

[30] A third culture child is one who seeks to bring together their parents' culture with a new host culture, thus forming an adapted third culture which is neither the parents' nor the host culture's as such.

children produces a new relationship which in turn forms a new culture within the family. The cultures of both parent and child are imperfect in terms of adaptation to the host culture. The transformation required to transition into a new family culture demands a high degree of negotiation and other skills, such as relational and emotional intelligence.

The implication of this transition clearly reveals that continuing to establish old-pattern monoculture communities cannot be sustained, because society is currently developing into a new culture that is multi-ethnic in appearance, with people who migrate and make their homes in the West and to some degree adopt the Western culture and its perspective. It would seem appropriate to consider that the formation of multi-ethnic congregations will require an organic and flexible attitude. An organic approach allows people time to adjust to each other interculturally, as well as to creatively experiment with how to relate to each other, worship together and enjoy fellowship in meaningful ways together.

Children from such a third-culture perspective will also relate to peers from the host culture who are themselves from a monocultural background. In the process, both sets of children encounter a liminal adaptive cultural context, which contributes to the formation of an emerging culture unknown to both sets of parents, but which contributes to a newly developing North European culture. This may prove to be a vital missional bridge that culturally intelligent missional strategists, including 'reverse missionaries' and host culture churches, should embrace and utilise in their multicultural churches.

The Homogenous Unit Principle

During the past fifty years, many authors have explored ideas of church growth, and many church planters have debated how churches can grow more quickly. One of the most enthusiastic was the missiologist Dr Donald McGavran, who proposed the Homogenous Unit Principle (HUP). This is the notion that evangelism is most successful among and between people of similar sociocultural backgrounds. This theory offers insights into how monocultural communities can grow quickly – growth that can become a starting point for the development of multi-ethnic, multicultural communities for mission. There are examples of the application of the HUP in the New Testament, which are relevant to the Church today and its relationship to the multi-ethnic community. These examples raise issues regarding the relationship between gospel and culture and the place that numerical growth has in church-planting issues.

Donald McGavran was researching the reasons for church growth and noted that churches grew more quickly where the people were from a single culture. Sociologically he found that in secular society, people come together on the basis of race, language, age, workplace or social class. He applied this idea to the Church and found that churches grow more quickly if their members have many characteristics in common. From this he formulated his Homogeneous Unit Principle as a basis for church growth.[31]

---

[31] Donald McGavran, *Understanding Church Growth* (Grand Rapids, MI: Eerdmans, 1990), p153.

All those whom Christ called as His first disciples were from His home area, some were related to each other and all were Jews. It was only later that the Church developed wider relationships as it grew. Arguably, most of the early churches were homogenous Jewish fellowships. It was only after Peter and Paul began to cross cultural barriers that Gentiles joined with Jews in fellowship together.

In today's context, many church planters have adopted the Homogenous Unit Principle and similarly concentrate their efforts on one segment of society. The characteristics that inform the homogenous unit are transferable to the monocultural community. Monocultural communities can be defined by their commonalities, such as shared ethnicity, culture and values. A clear, observable feature in church growth today is that migrant churches are not often set up mainly on social or economic terms, but mainly on cultural and ethnic associations – like the host culture churches, they are not multi-ethnic or multicultural. Yet the emerging UK culture is neither British nor immigrant, but a new, third-culture incarnation.

Despite the successful application of the HUP in many places, it also has its critics. The missiologist Peter Wagner has said that this model is by far the most controversial of all church growth principles, with its emphasis on numerical growth and on evangelising a single group of people. Some of McGavran's critics feel it is a denial of the universality of the gospel.[32]

This principle also brings into question the relationship of the gospel to the surrounding culture. The New

[32] C Peter Wagner, *Church Growth and the Whole Gospel* (Bromley: MARC Europe, 1981), p166.

Testament displays a number of approaches to addressing this relationship, the most notable of which are the struggles of the Jerusalem church with the Judaisers, Paul's sermon in Athens, and his disagreement with Peter when, as recorded in Galatians, he came to the church at Antioch (Galatians 2:11).

Homogenous versus heterogeneous

There is sharp controversy in church-planting circles over the relationship between a homogeneous unit as opposed to a heterogeneous unit approach.

A heterogeneous approach allows for more than one cultural group to interact as they try to creatively understand their differences, accept otherness and unite in their diversity, seeking to maximise their strengths and to minimise the possibilities of conflict. Advocates of a heterogeneous approach claim that the apostolic movement in the New Testament aimed to break down the barrier between Jews and Gentiles, between slaves and free, and between male and female. The early Church proclaimed the gospel to Jews and Gentiles together, and this preaching involved a call to be incorporated into a sociologically mixed Church. The Church grew across cultural barriers and each congregation was called to express unity in Christ across natural social divisions. After an initial ideological struggle, crossing cultural norms came to be part of New Testament church life and was regarded as essential. For Paul, becoming a believer was to enter a new humanity – he even says a new world, or 'new creation'[33] – although initially from a monocultural background. Entering a new creation means that homogenous groupings for the sake of growth are not a biblical alternative.

In his *Body Politics*,[34] the ethicist and theologian Howard Yoder argues that in Paul's thought, baptism brings the New Testament Church from a monocultural to a multicultural reality. In the early days of the Church in Jerusalem, there was a dispute between Hebraic Jewish widows and Hellenic Jewish widows (Acts 6:1). Although they shared the same faith and were 'Jewish', they came from different cultural backgrounds and spoke different languages. Some were Aramaic-speaking and some were Greek-speaking, and this must have caused difficulties. The Church's answer was to appoint seven men, all of whom had Greek names. This helped to balance the stronger Jewish influence in the Church.[35]

As the Church developed, Paul addressed this and other issues in some of his letters. First, he tackled the fundamental division of Jew versus Gentile. Paul wrote to the Ephesians that the 'wall of hostility' that used to separate Jew and Gentile had been 'broken down' (Ephesians 2:14).

Secondly, he addressed the division of social class. The early Church contained both the rich and the poor, the

[33] 2 Corinthians 5:17.

[34] John Howard Yoder, *Body Politics: Five Practices of the Christian Community Before the Watching World* (Scottdale, PA: Herald Press, 1992), p37.

[35] E H Trenchard, 'Acts', G C D Howley, ed, *A New Testament Commentary* (London: Pickering and Inglis, 1969), p302.

educated and the ignorant. As Paul reminded the Corinthians, 'Remember, dear brothers and sisters, that few of you were wise in the world's eyes or powerful or wealthy when God called you' (1 Corinthians 1:26, NLT).

Thirdly, he addressed the barrier of social standing. In Paul's churches, both slaves and their masters were members of the same fellowship. Paul gave instructions to both when he wrote, 'Slaves, obey your earthly masters … masters, treat your slaves in the same way' (Ephesus 6:5,9, NIV UK).

Fourthly, gender was a contentious issue that Paul dealt with. The New Testament Church welcomed both men and women, which is evident from Paul's letter to the Galatians: 'There is neither Jew nor Greek, there is neither slave nor free, there is no male and female, for you are all one in Christ Jesus' (Galatians 3:28).

Despite the emphasis on an inclusive, heterogeneous Church, it should be recognised that when each church was planted, it was probably a homogenous unit. When Paul arrived in a new location, he usually started his ministry among the Jews. For example, in Corinth, he 'reasoned in the synagogue … and tried to persuade Jews and Greeks' (Acts 18:4). And in Thessalonica, he went straight to the Jewish synagogue and, 'as was his custom … reasoned with them from the Scriptures' (Acts 17:2).

The synagogues in Corinth and Thessalonica were examples of diaspora Judaism which attracted mixed congregations. They were composed of God-fearers, proselytes and ethnic Jews. They were united in their adherence to Judaism and, in this sense, were a homogeneous unit. It was to their Jewish background that

Paul directed his message, although they were ethnically mixed. However, even in this image of the churches planted by Paul, the shift to the multi-ethnic church can be seen. The gospel was already reaching out to a multicultural community, adding to the existing monocultural community of the Jewish people. The ethnic mix was already an indication of the future community of God. Diaspora Jewish people did not become extinct, but rather grew because a variety of different cultures was added to them. In similar vein, the contemporary multicultural West will now witness the growth of multi-ethnic churches.

Numerical growth as a kingdom issue

One might ask, why it is that some churches seem to be growing and doing very well while other churches are in decline? McGavran suggested that finding the right strategy is crucial for church growth. He went on to suggest that the Homogenous Unit Principle was the best way of achieving growth, and that it is essential for the initiators to be of the unit themselves for churches to grow.

From the beginning of the church growth movement, increase in numbers was seen as a key indicator of health. McIntosh highlights a statement made by Glasser: 'God wills the growth of His church … The church that does not grow is out of the will of God.'[36] But the question then needs to be asked, 'Should growth be the foundational

---

[36] Gary McIntosh, *Evaluating the Church Growth Movement* (Grand Rapids, MI: Zondervan, 2004), pp182-183.

focus of the church?'[37] The New Testament records that the early Church in Jerusalem grew from twelve to 120 and then 3,000 on the day of Pentecost. From there it multiplied into other countries and cultures. The measurement of numerical growth alone has been criticised as being insufficient, but it is a misunderstanding to assume that the strategy of the church growth movement is restricted to numerical growth. Charles van Engel points out, 'One concept has been consistently offered: that numerical growth is only a thermometer, a symptom, an indicator, of other issues at work in the life of the church.'[38] Christian Schwartz is quoted by van Engel as criticising the emphasis on numerical growth:

> Large numbers of publications on the theology behind church growth were surprisingly one-sided in their focus on the aspect of numerical growth ... Numerical growth seems to me to be a side issue – albeit an important one – of church development. It is not the strategic goal, but one of many natural consequences of a church's health is to experience growth.[39]

Donald McGavran himself accepted that numerical growth is a means to mission and not an end in itself. The reason he said this is because the more people who join a faith community, the more people there are to participate in the work of mission. Church growth therefore means

---

[37] McIntosh, *Evaluating the Church Growth Movement*, p156.

[38] McIntosh, *Evaluating the Church Growth Movement*, p233.

[39] McIntosh, *Evaluating the Church Growth Movement*, pp144-145.

more than numerical growth. A large church is not necessarily a strong church. It may just be a fat church. To say that a church is big does not necessarily mean that it is healthy, if mission is not at its heart.

So how can church growth be measured, if not numerically? Some numerically large churches today make the mistake of believing that because of their size they do not need partnerships, nor to enter into a working relationship with small churches. Such churches may be in danger of suffering from the terminal disease of pride. A church can grow in other ways than in simple numbers. One useful analysis is offered by Elmer Towns. He shows that these include internal growth, meaning 'qualitative growth in the Word of God, in the Lord, in grace, and in spiritual maturity', and numerical growth that includes biological, conversion and transfer growth. [40] However, Clive Jarvis argues:

> there cannot be any substantial difficulty in accepting [Donald McGavran's] central thesis that God intends for his church to grow numerically as well as spiritually and maturely. [41]

McGavran, in his foreword to the church growth writers Yamamori and Lawson's book on introducing church growth, criticised those who say, 'We are not growing in numbers but we are in quality,' by stating that this is an

[40] McIntosh, *Evaluating the Church Growth Movement*, pp44-45.
[41] Clive Jarvis, *Church Growth Revisited*, unpublished manuscript available in the library of Springdale College, p5.

unconvincing cop-out.[42] This is an acceptable criticism, as church growth in the Bible is seen in two dimensions: numerical and spiritual. The quality of the spiritual life of a church should naturally result in numerical growth as people from outside are attracted to the church. This was the case of the early Church in Jerusalem as they 'devoted themselves to the apostles' teaching and to fellowship, to the breaking of bread and to prayer' (Acts 2:42, NIV UK). The result was that 'the Lord added to their number daily those who were being saved' (Acts 2:47, NIV UK). A theological critique may be added here to the effect that it was not the Church that caused people to join it, but it was the Lord at work through His Spirit who added to their numbers. In other words, church growth is a divine action which people can participate in encouraging, but for anyone to become a real converted believer is first and foremost God's work.

McIntosh highlights the importance of qualitative growth and quotes Carl Holladay, who says:

> Numerical growth was not a pervasive concern of Jesus and the New Testament Writers. Only Luke with his fondness for statistics documents the numerical growth of the early Christian church.[43]

However, the Gospel writers record that Jesus was concerned to reach as many people as possible. He taught

---

[42] Tetsunao Yamamori and LeRoy Lawson, *Introducing Church Growth* (Cincinnati, OH: Standard Publishing, 1975), pV.

[43] McIntosh, *Evaluating the Church Growth Movement*, p183.

the multitudes and later commissioned His disciples to go into all the world, literally, to all people groups (Matthew 28:19).

The importance of numerical growth is a challenge to the Church today, particularly in these days of decline in Western churches. Martin Robinson and Dwight Smith are deeply concerned with this question, as they ask, 'Where have all the people gone?'[44]

McGavran's concern is just as relevant today. Clive Jarvis, the church growth writer, states, 'It is the challenge to realize that, however we define the purposes of God, we must include numerical growth as a priority.'[45]

Gospel and culture

McGavran's HUP necessarily assumes an interaction with a monocultural community. The early Church spread among the predominantly Jewish communities in the Middle East. The culture, with its Jewish background, was sympathetic to the new faith, because the roots of Christianity were in the Jewish Scriptures, the Old Testament. At the same time, the gospel naturally embraces people of all cultures: Jesus commanded His disciples to 'go therefore and make disciples of all nations' (Matthew 28:19).

The making of disciples means that it is a process of people becoming increasingly like Christ on a qualitative level. Hence church growth through church planting cannot be done in isolation from an effective discipleship

---

[44] Robinson and Smith, *Invading Secular Space*, p15.

[45] Jarvis, *Church Growth Revisited*, p5.

process that equips ordinary people to become disciple-makers as well. Of course, important for this book is the fact that disciples are to be made from peoples from all nations. This assumes that the messengers will cross national and ethnic boundaries, and that the message will be relevant to all, whatever their language or culture. Paul believed that the gospel would be effective in any culture, that it would always do what it said it would do: 'For I am not ashamed of the gospel, for it is the power of God for salvation to everyone who believes, to the Jew first and also to the Greek' (Romans 1:16). Christians look forward to the time when 'every knee [will] bow ... and every tongue acknowledge that Jesus Christ is Lord' (Philippians 2:10-11, NIV UK), and to heaven, which will be filled with those 'from every nation, tribe, people and language' (Revelation 7:9, NIV UK).

However, if people are to believe, the message must be understood before it can touch their hearts. When facing the Athenians, who had no background in the Jewish faith, Paul recognised the need to adapt his preaching, and he quoted from some of their own poets (Acts 17:28). Some critics think that Paul was mistaken in adapting his message in this way, but in fact he was only using the local culture as an illustration. He was successful, as verse 34 shows: 'some joined him and became believers' (NLT) – quite a successful outcome among philosophers!

It is quite plain to see that Paul's dexterity, delicacy and sensitivity in dealing with people from cultures other than his own were essential ingredients in the effective development of multicultural communities for mission. But a wider question needs to be addressed: whether the gospel is identically compatible with every culture. Surely, within each culture, not all aspects are neutral or good, and so some elements will need transforming.

Culture and Christianity

Like Paul, church planters today need to minimise the hurdles that new believers need to jump. These will include barriers caused by obvious differences, such as ethnicity, colour, tribe, religion and language, to mention but a few. Naturally, people have a great attachment to their own culture, and it can be very difficult for them to leave parts of it. Becoming a Christian involves a radical change of direction: 'conversion'. But where the gospel does not conflict with a person's culture, it is unnecessary to pursue changes that are simply cosmetic.

Unfortunately, in the past, mission has often been linked with colonialism, and bearers of the gospel have imported their own culture. For example, in nineteenth-century rural Africa, churches with wooden pews and stained-glass windows were built, totally out of keeping with the local scene. As the Lausanne Covenant noted in 1974, 'Missions have all too frequently exported with the Gospel an alien culture, and churches have sometimes been in bondage to culture rather than to the Scripture.'[46]

The challenge to Christians who share the good news is to ensure that the message is free from unnecessary cultural baggage which hinders the spread of the gospel. When the gospel is accompanied by such conditions, those

---

[46] J D Douglas, *Let The Earth Hear His Voice* (Minneapolis, MN: World Wide Publications 1975), p7.

being evangelised can fear that if they become Christians, they will be rejected by their own people. McGavran offered two examples: the Orthodox Jews and the caste system in India. Both have a high consciousness of their own people group, which will lead to resistance to the gospel primarily because, to these people, becoming a Christian means joining another culture.[47]

McGavran showed that people groups become Christian fastest when the least change is involved. He quoted Lyle Schaller's research which found that of those who had joined the church over a ten-year period, up to 90 per cent were brought by a friend or relative, namely 'people like us'.[48] McGavran also quoted research that shows that the few converts who have started large group movements have deliberately continued as part of their own group. They continue to love their people, serve them and identify with them to prove that they are still good members of society.[49] Therefore, in transitioning from a monocultural community to developing a multi-ethnic missional community, church planters who enable people to become Christians without the need to cross cultural barriers are likely to be more effective than those who place barriers in their way. In this sense, the multi-ethnic community makes no demand upon other cultures in terms of rejecting them or treating them as inferior; rather, it embraces this cultural diversity even as a tool to reach more people.

---

[47] McGavran, *Understanding Church Growth*, p155.

[48] McGavran, *Understanding Church Growth*, p165.

[49] McGavran, *Understanding Church Growth*, p173.

Few would disagree that the Homogeneous Unit Principle is effective in initial evangelism. However, experience shows that many churches move on to become heterogeneous. In the UK today, most cities are multi-ethnic. People of different nationalities and traditions are living side by side. However, the 'pull' of ethnic and religious ties means that people will gravitate to others who are similar to them, hence the monocultural church. These groups can be reached with the gospel using the HUP, but it means that native British Christians in the UK must cross cultural barriers and share the gospel in ways that fit with non-British cultures and vice versa – both need to prepare multi-ethnic communities for successful mission.

As time goes on, monocultural immigrant communities change as they learn English and their children start to forget their native languages. An example are the Welsh churches in Liverpool. They were founded early in the twentieth century when Welsh miners came to work there. Fifty years later, in the 1960s, there were about eighteen churches but all their members were elderly, since the next generation had not learned Welsh. Today only two churches remain. Because they did not move on to become heterogeneous communities, the majority died.

The same danger faces immigrant communities in the UK today. First-generation immigrants tend to hold on to their own culture, become trapped in a monocultural community and cease to grow numerically. As they become more 'Westernised', second- or third-generation immigrants are less likely to be bound by 'people consciousness'. While still retaining something of their own culture, migrant churches need to move to the stage of becoming multi-ethnic communities for mission, and to take their place in the wider British Church scene rather than being separate from it.

Cultural diversity among the early Christians

Jesus was a Jew, His first followers were Jews, and the Church was initially born as a Jewish offshoot. In its infancy, straight after Pentecost, the early Church was monocultural. However, there was some cultural variety in the Church from the very beginning: on the day of Pentecost, there were Jews from the Dispersion present, and proselytes too. Acts 2:5 records, 'Now there were staying in Jerusalem God-fearing Jews from every nation under heaven' (NIV UK). They became disciples and returned to their countries of origin with their new-found faith.

Meanwhile, the Jerusalem church lost its Hellenist wing and became the repository of a strictly Jewish Christianity. The Jerusalem conference in Acts 15 decided against this conservative group of Judaisers. The New Testament scholar T W Manson observes, 'This Jewish Christianity had no future. It maintained itself for a long time, but ... from the beginning of the second century ... it dwindled and disappeared.'[50] The Church crossed further cultural barriers as a result of the persecution that arose following the death of Stephen (Acts 8:1), when 'the refugees of the

---

[50] T W Manson, *A Companion to the Bible* (Edinburgh: T&T Clark, 1950), p396.

Hellenist party dispersed, preaching their version of the faith to all corners of the Roman Empire'.[51]

The next major development was the beginning of the mission to the Gentiles. This started with Peter's vision of the folded sheet, and then his preaching to the household of Cornelius (Acts 10). The door for Gentiles to enter the Church had been opened. Paul then took up the challenge and, despite his strong Jewish background and training, became the apostle to the Gentiles.

As Paul and his companions set off on their missionary journeys to evangelise and to plant churches, they showed their respect for the culture in which the gospel was born. When arriving at a new place they often first went to the synagogue. For example, when they arrived in Salamis they proclaimed the word of God in the Jewish synagogues. Their motto was 'to the Jew first', but if rejected they moved from the synagogue and started churches that met in the houses of Gentile believers. For example, in Corinth, when the Jews opposed Paul and became abusive, he shook out his clothes in protest and said to them, 'From now on I will go to the Gentiles' (Acts 18:6). Then he left the synagogue and went next door to the house of Titius Justus who was 'a worshipper of God' (verse 7). The same thing happened in Ephesus, when Paul left the synagogue after teaching there for three months and moved his discussions to the lecture hall of Tyrannus. As a result 'all the Jews and Greeks who lived in the province of Asia heard the word of the Lord' (Acts 19:10, NIV UK). This demonstrated the cross-cultural appeal of

---

[51] Manson, *A Companion to the Bible*, p395.

the gospel and the need to develop the missional multicultural community.

Paul's strategy was a precursor of McGavran's church growth principle of concentrating gospel effort on the place where the people are most responsive. But Paul realised that the process had to culminate in a missional multicultural community. If a monocultural community persistently rejects the gospel, it is better to adopt the same attitude as Paul and shake the dust from our feet and go to where the gospel will get a hearing and be received.

However, Paul's policy was not 'either/or' but 'both/and'. His heart-cry, as apostle to the Gentiles in Romans 9–11, was for the Jewish people to be saved. He was concerned that both Jew and Gentile should be part of the multicultural body of Christ, the Church.

From the beginning, it wasn't easy for the Church to be multicultural. All the indications in the New Testament are that the early Jewish Christian communities used largely Jewish forms in which to express their new faith in Jesus. Then later, in Gentile contexts, the Church began to borrow from Greek culture. Some scholars argue that early Gentile forms of the Church borrowed from the political structures of the Greek city-states.

At Antioch, differences arose about the extent to which Jewish and Gentile believers should intermingle, and this developed into a major split between Peter and Paul, in which Paul accused Barnabas and Peter of hypocrisy (Galatians 2). Manson points out:

> For Paul, there was no half-way house. Either Gentiles were to be admitted unconditionally to full Christian fellowship, or the Church was still

essentially a Jewish institution, and this was to him a misunderstanding of the Gospel.[52]

Paul thus shows that the gospel supersedes culture.

Culture in the New Testament

The New Testament shows that the gospel is for all people, regardless of background and culture. Jesus told the disciples to take this message to all nations. Humankind is created in the image of God, and therefore every culture which develops will have many good, God-like elements in it. But because of the Fall, sin has corrupted humanity and therefore culture is corrupted too. Paul makes this clear in Romans 1 where he states that the whole of humankind is under God's wrath, 'without excuse' (verse 20). He goes on to condemn all sorts of practices that can arise in every culture. He shows that the antidote for sin is the message of the gospel: 'the power of God for salvation to everyone who believes, to the Jew first and also to the Greek' (verse 16).

The gospel crosses cultural barriers and reaches all segments of society. The message that in Christ there is neither 'Greek nor Jew, circumcised or uncircumcised, barbarian, Scythian, slave or free, but Christ is all and in all' (Colossians 3:11, NET) cuts right across the social and religious norms of the day. Thus, the New Testament Church unites believers from different cultures, without passing judgement on their background. But the gospel of love goes further, in that it encourages Christians to respect

---

[52] Manson, *A Companion to the Bible*, p398.

each other's cultural differences without offence. In his teaching on food sacrificed to idols (1 Corinthians 8–10), Paul reminds his readers that 'Everything is permissible – but not everything is beneficial' (1 Corinthians 10:23, NIV 1984), and ends with the command: 'Do not cause anyone to stumble, whether Jews, Greeks or the church of God' (verse 32, NIV UK).

To sum up

Ultimately, it is not so much a matter of principle as to whether we use a homogenous approach or a heterogeneous approach, because both are found in the New Testament, and both are effective. It is more a matter of strategy. The gospel is God's salvation plan for the whole world, so it cannot differentiate between cultures; it regards all cultures, and all the people within them, as equally tainted by sin and equally in need of redemption.

The gospel is above culture. Jesus was born as a Jew into a specific culture which God had prepared to reach out to all nations. He was to be a light to the Gentiles as well as the glory of His people Israel. Through His death on the cross, He broke down the wall separating Jew and Gentile, and therefore the message of the gospel applies to the whole world. Jesus emphasised this when commissioning His disciples before He ascended (Matthew 28:19). Again, this shows that the gospel is above culture.

However, in the initial proclamation of the gospel in an unreached area, it may well be strategic to concentrate on an individual culture by targeting one specific group. This must be done with care. If a specific group is targeted, there is the danger of adapting the message, deliberately or by mistake, to fit that culture in a way that denies the fullness of the gospel and perhaps avoids the offence of the cross. This adaptation contains the twin dangers of neglecting or ignoring certain aspects of a culture which conflict with the gospel in an effort to be relevant or, conversely, unnecessarily imposing a foreign culture on a different people group because it seems expedient to do so.

Church growth statistics show the effectiveness of the Homogeneous Unit Principle today, and New Testament evidence shows that the Church grew in this way in its early stages. But Jesus' command to go to all people groups, and Paul's theology of no cultural barriers in Christ challenges churches planted as homogeneous units to move to become heterogeneous. John Stott points out that because Christ has broken down all dividing walls, 'we must declare that a homogeneous church is a defective church, which must work penitently and perseveringly towards heterogeneity'.[53]

The thrust of this book is that the time for mono-ethnic church planting is passing, as in a multicultural society people will increasingly interact with each other across ethnicities and cultures, meaning that more heterogeneous faith communities will need to come into existence. Now is the appointed time for culturally intelligent leaders to shift from monocultural communities and embark unreservedly on planting and developing multi-ethnic communities for mission. This is in keeping with the final picture of the Church that the book of Revelation gives, of a vast congregation drawn from 'every nation, from all

---

[53] John Stott, *The Message of Romans* (Leicester: IVP, 1994), p398.

tribes and peoples and languages' (7:9) praising God together, with all barriers removed.

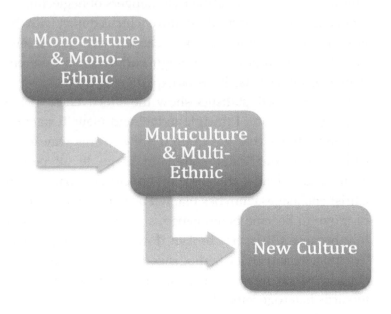

Reflection

- *Why is the Homogeneous Unit Principle effective in diaspora evangelism?*

- *What are its limitations for reaching the host community with the gospel?*

- *Outline your strategy for reaching the host culture in the UK. What steps would you need to take for these plans to be effective?*

Chapter Five

Establishing Multi-ethnic Missional Communities in a New Culture Context

Without going into much debate, it is my assumption that church planting is a necessary part of the *missio Dei*. It is about church growth and expansion, increasing and taking over new ground, opening the gospel to as many people as possible. The time has come for even the natural composition and outlook of the Church itself to shift to a new level of being God's community. This is the key area for developing and building multi-ethnic communities for mission. Soon, multi-ethnic churches will come about naturally as the current generation of children grows up and becomes a significant sector of society. However, this assumption depends upon our ability to retain our children and young people as engaged and effective members of the Church, who are committed to mission.

We have already seen that, owing to population movements and immigrant churches growing as children are born to members, the UK's population is becoming significantly more ethnically mixed. In the past, immigrant churches were planted only in the big cosmopolitan cities as immigrants felt compelled to move to these cities to maintain their identity, but nowadays, as they begin to be welcomed into local communities, they are being incorporated if not entirely assimilated into home churches. For instance, during my recent visit to a congregation in Rochdale, a small northern industrial town, I was amazed to see an almost equal representation of African, Asian and British people. The senior pastor said that this happened naturally after the church welcomed and supported the first few families, who then attracted other families. I also noticed that the number of children was probably the same as that of the adults which, of course, was representative of the different ethnicities of the parents. I began to realise that, given their ethnic and cultural mix, they are developing a new, shared culture. As the children grow up together, they will forge a new, common culture that is influenced by their diverse and contrasting backgrounds.

In this church, there was one young Ethiopian called Abel Engeda, who has great potential to build a bridge between his parents' culture and the developing host culture. This young man has a strong passion for young people in general from any cultural background, and because of his cultural intelligence, he is able to relate to many of them. It was heartening to see that he has been included in the leadership team of the church.

I have known quite a few young Ethiopian people like him in the UK, other parts of Europe, the USA and Australia. In my research in 2012 for 'The Development of Ethiopian and Eritrean Evangelical Churches in the UK: Missional movement or Cultural Dead-end?',[54] a key

[54] Hirpo Kumbi, 'The Development Of Ethiopian And Eritrean Evangelical Churches In The United Kingdom: Missional

finding was the passion that Ethiopian leaders living in the West have to reach out to other cultural groups. More than fifty key leaders interviewed shared their sense of strong calling to help in the facilitation of effective mission across all cultures in society. A barrier they discussed was a need for the people of their diaspora to effectively communicate in the English language, or other languages appropriate to the people group(s) they might seek to work with. This desire to work missionally with other people groups is well expressed by the young people I have mentioned. They seek to make themselves available to work alongside different churches, in order to help them bridge cultural gaps. This willingness is important to note, and we need to actively encourage younger adults like them to exercise their considerable gifts as relational, cross-cultural bridge builders.

Current churches can take the first step to becoming 'bridge culture churches' by initially gathering another ethnic group. In this role, a church becomes a bridge from the traditional monocultural setting towards developing a new cultural perspective. To develop into a bridge culture church, it is necessary to attract relevant people or groups into this new culture. Such a culture would comprise third-culture youths combined with interested host culture and immigrant young adults.

Host culture youths and their faith communities who interact with third-culture youth and children have, in some cases known to me, meaningfully accepted each other's cultural differences and interact well together. The

Movement Or Cultural Dead-end?' Masters dissertation, University of Wales, 2012.

outcome of these engagements is a new, dynamic, emerging culture. This new culture is not static, as it continues to reform and reshape itself as the various interchanges form new norms. This new culture defies old paradigms and is only comfortable in communities ready for mission. This is because of the sense of 'buy-in' that communities which have embraced a desire to find fresh ways of existing together have, meaning that they commit to the challenges that change brings. If there is not 'buy-in', it is less likely that people in communities will tolerate some necessary effort and pain in order to successfully negotiate intercultural community life.

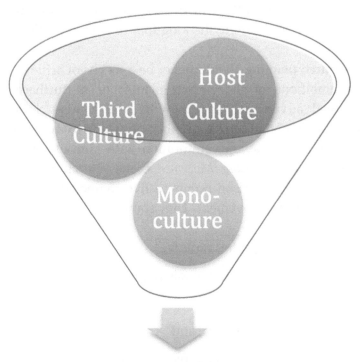

New Culture

Peter Wagner famously said that church planting is the single most effective means of evangelism available to us. However, church planting is *not* simply evangelism; rather, it is evangelism with a purpose. Church planting is the heart of mission, since it is about purposefully establishing faith communities that grow out of and focus upon disciple-making. Church planting does not come out of the acquisition of a specific set of skills, useful as these skills may be for the process; rather, it is a means of converting non-believers and forming them into new communities of faith, which arise out of a vision and passion for establishing the kingdom of God in particular settings.

Church planting should never be a means of achieving the ambitions of the church planter or of furthering personal advantage. God may be said to use church planting as one among a number of means to draw lost persons into a saving communion with Himself. In his book, *Church Planting Movements*, the church planting thinker David Garrison points to five characteristics of a church planting movement. They should:

- reproduce churches rapidly,

- multiply to reach the whole population,

- be indigenous,

- reproduce themselves, and

- operate within local people groups.[55]

The idea of church planting comes from Christ's own command to go into all the world and 'make disciples of all nations, baptizing them in the name of the Father and of the Son and of the Holy Spirit' (Mathew 28:19). The Greek term often translated 'all nations' in this passage is *ta ethene*, better rendered 'people groups', since it does not indicate a geo-political entity in the modern sense, but rather any distinct cultural and/or linguistic group that has its own identity. Christ's global disciple-making mandate

---

[55] Garrison, *Church Planting Movements*, p21.

by its nature carries multi-ethnic overtones. Moreover, the fact that these new disciples are to be baptised into the threefold name of God suggests that the process of disciple-making focuses on creating community rather than merely saving individuals. From the outset, evangelisation was focused on the kind of communal life characterised by the Godhead, so it is important to see individuals not only converted, but also gathered together in worshipping communities.

Robinson observes in his *Planting Mission-Shaped Churches Today*[56] that the need for planting churches arises because many people in the West are not going to established churches.[57] Moreover, Brierley's most recent statistical analysis reveals that:

> although church membership in the UK is continuing to decline overall, the rate of decrease seems to have lessened significantly, with the result that the membership level previously anticipated for 2020 will probably not now be evident until 2025. Moreover, the trend is bucked in Independent, New, Orthodox, and Pentecostal Churches, as well as in the category of smaller bodies, all of which reported absolute growth

---

[56] Martin Robinson, *Planting Mission-Shaped Churches Today* (Oxford: Monarch, 2006), p30.

[57] Peter Brierley, *The Tide is Running Out, Christian Research*, 2000.

between 2008 and 2013, much of which can be attributed to the effects of immigration.[58]

Nevertheless, the overall picture is depressing. In *The Death of Christianity in Britain* the historian Callum Brown reported:

> The cycle of the renewal of Christianity was dramatically broken in the 1960s ... It took several centuries to convert Britain to Christianity, but it has taken less than forty years for the country to forsake it.[59]

The decline of Christianity in Western countries is a cause for alarm, hence the need for re-evangelisation focused on the planting of new churches. To be sustainable in the longer term, owing to the cultural changes in Britain, the objective should be to actively seek engagement with all cultures in a healthy realisation of multi-ethnic missional community as described earlier in this book.

Healthy church replication

The healthy replication of new churches is an essential criterion of the success of a church plant. The health of a church is best evaluated by its sending capability to plant more churches. Rick Warren points out, 'A Church's health

---

[58] Clive D Field, 'Second Edition of UK Church Statistics', British Religion in Numbers, 3rd October 2014, available at: www.brin.ac.uk/2014/second-edition-of-uk-church-statistics/ (accessed 23rd June 2017).

[59] Quoted in Robinson and Smith, *Invading Secular Space*, p21.

is measured by its sending capacity, not its seating capacity.'[60]

Robinson highlights the importance of church planting in this way: 'Church planting is a natural part of the redefinition of the over-all make-up of the church.'[61] Put simply, church planting is meant to be part of the Church's DNA – the Church is born to reproduce.

The church planting specialist Stetzer suggests:

> Church planting should not end with the establishment of one church. The process can repeat itself ... The kingdom is best advanced through multiplication and not just addition.[62]

Stetzer goes on to point out that if a new church does not plant another church within three years, it likely never will.[63] However, this view has a degree of cultural bias to it, in the sense that this may only be true in the context of certain types of churches. It does not follow that a new church can be so speedily established in a late modern context where it takes much longer to disciple new believers. Hence three years may turn into five years.

The key person in this multiplication process is the original church planter, who must have the vision to plant yet more churches. Stetzer suggests, 'The planter initiates

---

[60] Rick Warren, *The Purpose Driven Church* (Grand Rapids, MI: Zondervan, 1995), p32.

[61] Robinson, *Planting Mission-Shaped Churches Today*, p30.

[62] Ed Stetzer, *Planting Missional Churches* (Nashville, TN: B&H Publishing Group, 2006), p316.

[63] Stetzer, *Planting Missional Churches*, p317.

a daughter church by casting a church planting vision.'[64] The planter is someone who has been called into church planting by God, and has church planting in their DNA; they have the gift for it, so will want to move on and plant new churches. Again, Stetzer comments:

> The entrepreneurial planter is usually an innovative and enthusiastic person who continually seeks a new challenge that sometimes involves moving to a new church plant every few years.[65]

Firstly, the planter must communicate the vision to the new church. It may come as a shock to the young church to be challenged at the outset to think already of becoming a planting church themselves. The church planting writers Gibbs and Coffey point out, 'Churches living out the apostolic paradigm define themselves in missional terms and are prepared to embark upon risk-taking initiatives.'[66]

Secondly, the young church needs to develop leaders who will have the gifts and training both to carry on the work of the existing church and to move on to the next church plant. Stetzer suggests:

> One crucial imperative of new churches is leadership development ... many pastors and planters testify that as their churches have commissioned leaders and sent them out, God

[64] Stetzer, *Planting Missional Churches*, p316.

[65] Stetzer, *Planting Missional Churches*, p69.

[66] Eddie Gibbs and Ian Coffey, *Church Next* (Westmont, IL: IVP, 2001), p226.

has replaced those leaders and allowed even more people to become involved in the leadership core of the church.[67]

Thirdly, a team with appropriate gifts should be appointed by the church to take responsibility for the new church plant. 'Another step towards planting is the church's appointment of a planting leadership team that is empowered to establish new multi-cultural congregations.'[68] This team will need training in the various crucial ministries in the new church. For example, even Christians who are natural evangelists can benefit from special training, especially in appreciating cultural diversity and working within a multicultural community context. 'Their natural giftedness can be enhanced by specific training.'[69]

> Church planting movements are not in full flower until the churches begin spontaneously reproducing themselves ... one church planter explained, 'When I see a church that I helped start reproduce a daughter church which itself reproduces a new church that produces yet another church, I know I have done my job'.[70]

Thus, we see that church plants must reproduce themselves, or they will eventually die. This can be seen

---

[67] Stetzer, *Planting Missional Churches*, p318.

[68] Stetzer, *Planting Missional Churches*, p317.

[69] Martin Robinson, *To Win The West* (Oxford: Monarch, 1996), p209.

[70] Garrison, *Church Planting Movements*, p193.

among many churches in Britain, for example, where congregations have become elderly and energy has been lost to cultivate numerical growth by seeing new converts join them. Church planting is one recognised way to refresh growth, where, among other approaches, new churches are planted alongside ageing congregations, meaning that the elderly can be cared for pastorally, and fresh churches with new members will provide younger people to support new and older congregations alike.

Identification of leaders

Having people willing to go is a key element for successful church planting. Paul says in Romans 10:15:

> how are they to preach unless they are sent? As it is written, 'How beautiful are the feet of those who preach the good news!'

and Isaiah 6:8 says:

> And I heard the voice of the Lord saying, 'Whom shall I send, and who will go for us?' Then I said, 'Here am I! Send me.'

In Paul's own missionary journey, he changed direction when he had a vision one night of a Macedonian man begging him to 'Come over to Macedonia and help us'. In that way the gospel was brought to Europe for the first time (Acts 16:9).

The people seeking to take part in the church plant should be called by the Lord and respond to His call by joining the team proposing to plant the church. Then they should prepare themselves with suitable training. Jesus set the example by training His disciples for three years. This training involved both teaching from the Scriptures and practical instruction about how to do the work, and it was backed up by the personal example of Jesus Himself: 'he taught them as one who had authority, not as the scribes' (Mark 1:22).

Paul similarly taught fellow leaders such as Timothy and also gave them his own example to follow: 'You, however, have followed my teaching, my conduct, my aim in life, my faith, my patience, my love, my steadfastness, my persecutions and sufferings' (2 Timothy 3:10-11).

Finally, the planting team should be commissioned by the sending church: 'Then after fasting and praying they laid their hands on them and sent them off' (Acts 13:3).

Not all those who are willing to be part of a church planting team may be suitable. Leaders need to consider the personal qualities of each individual recruit, such as their character, their determination, their ability to work in team and, above all, spiritual qualities. As Paul points out to Timothy, 'what you have heard from me in the presence of many witnesses entrust to faithful men who will be able to teach others also' (2 Timothy 2:2). Paul was concerned that Timothy had the spiritual qualities necessary for his work: 'set the believers an example in speech, in conduct, in love, in faith, in purity' (1 Timothy 4:12).

It is very important to choose the right leaders with suitable gifts as they give direction to the new work and establish its character. They should be able to lay good foundations, always remembering that it is God's work to make it grow. As Paul says, 'I planted the seed, Apollos watered it, but God has been making it grow' (1 Corinthians 3:6, NIV UK).

Candidates for a church planting task should be mature believers, not recent converts. Mature believers are more likely to understand the message and its implications for a wide range of issues. In addition, they have a track record of following God. A prior history of relying on God's help is an important foundation for the future. This is what will see us through the tough times inevitably involved in the challenging work of church planting, where the devil will actively seek to destroy what we are doing.

Finally, the spiritual principle of sanctification tells us that our discipleship develops gradually over time. As time progresses we should make fewer mistakes and thus become more useful to God. Aspiring church planters should not be people who have a hidden agenda or people who want to leave the mother church because they are dissatisfied. Such people will only cause problems in the new church. Murray comments:

> The quality of these foundations has profound implications for what can be built on them. Strong and secure foundations provide the basis for healthy churches and effective mission. Weak and inadequate foundations jeopardize these prospects.[71]

In Ephesians 4, Paul shows that within the body of Christ, God assigns gifted individuals such as apostles,

---

[71] Stuart Murray, *Church Planting: Laying Foundations* (Carlisle: Paternoster Press, 1998), pXI.

prophets, evangelists, pastors and teachers to build up the whole body (Ephesians 4:11-12). These gifts need to be present in the planting team, as well as the basic gifts Paul mentions in his letter to the church at Corinth: those who have gifts of 'helping, administrating' (1 Corinthians 12:28).

It is important that the new church is managed in the right way, especially in the early days when new patterns are being developed and a new body of people is coming together. Robinson and Smith mention four management areas: 'Administration – the management of detail; Organization – the management of structure; Management – the management of people; and Leading – the management of the future.' [72] Additionally, in today's contemporary generation it is crucial to have an IT and media operations leader as well as the above.

For a healthy church plant, all these gifts need to be present and well balanced. Leaders need suitable gifts that complement each other and lead to the building-up of the church. Church planting is a team operation and therefore its leaders need to be able to lead a team rather than be brilliant individuals. Leaders should be people to whom others turn for encouragement and inspiration, who inspire confidence and hope, and who set an appropriate pace. 'Most leaders get the organization moving because of their energy and enthusiasm. The problem is most likely to be setting an unsustainable pace for the team and hence for the whole church.' [73]

---

[72] Robinson, *Planting Mission-Shaped Churches Today*, p89.
[73] Robinson, *Planting Mission-Shaped Churches Today*, p96.

Leaders also need to be able to prepare well and seek to minimise failure, and know how to manage it when it inevitably does happen. A study of 'leadership failures' can help to identify the key elements that should be present in the planting church.

Prayer and confirmation

Before starting the church plant, the first church members should spend much time in prayer. Prayer helps to prepare the hearts of the team who will be involved, and through prayer the Holy Spirit can guide and direct. The early Church set a good example from the beginning when they fasted and prayed before sending Saul and Barnabas off to Cyprus as the first missionaries: '"Set apart for me Barnabas and Saul for the work to which I have called them." Then after fasting and praying they laid their hands on them and sent them off' (Acts 13:2-3). Sometimes, through prayer and visions, God can change the direction of the thinking of the church planters. For example, as we have seen, Paul changed his direction after his vision of the man from Macedonia.

In all church planting, we must remember that God is sovereign and opens or closes the door. Prayer therefore ensures that church planters are in tune with God's mission and that the Holy Spirit is allowed to be the chief architect of the church planting enterprise. Commenting on his work in Ephesus, Paul said, 'a great door for effective work has opened to me, and there are many who oppose me' (1 Corinthians 16:9, NIV UK). This is the reality of developing a multi-ethnic missional community as exemplified by Paul, who realised and was obedient to this objective.

Prayer takes time, and very few church planters move quickly into planting. Speaking about the experience of many church planters, Robinson points out:

> They have almost all been able to point to a long process of prayer, answers to prayer, questioning, more prayer, some confirmation, and growing signs of being led to a particular path.[74]

The effect of prayer and seeking God's presence is an important foundation to the planting of any church for Christ as it shows our reliance on the Lord rather than on our own ideas and abilities. 'Not by might, nor by power, but by my Spirit, says the LORD of Hosts' (Zechariah 4:6). Paul requested prayer to enable him to preach the gospel, and he seems to have seen this as an element of spiritual warfare (Ephesians 6:18-19). Like the early disciples before Pentecost, church planters need to wait on the Lord for His direction and power (the power of the Holy Spirit) before they start to move into the new area: 'you will receive power when the Holy Spirit has come upon you' (Acts 1:8).

Locating church plants

Before selecting a geographical area for a new church plant, various factors need to be taken into consideration. The needs of the local people must be assessed, and it

---

[74] Robinson, *Planting Mission-Shaped Churches Today*, p65.

should be established whether any local churches are already meeting these needs. Much of the expansion of the early Church was spontaneous as the apostles were led by the Spirit, but even Paul did some research, as he records in Romans 15:20:

> It has always been my ambition to preach the gospel where Christ was not known, so that I would not be building on someone else's foundation. (NIV UK)

To establish a multi-ethnic church, the target area must be where multinationals live and its worship base should be easily accessible to the members. Jesus identified the areas in which His disciples should spread the gospel: 'you will be my witnesses in Jerusalem and in all Judea and Samaria, and to the end of the earth' (Acts 1:8). They started in Jerusalem because this was strategic. The decision about the place for the church plant is very important. 'The new church's location is like a hospital; it's where the birth of the new church happens.'[75]

Good preparation and research into the needs and demographic structure of the area needs to be undertaken, and a specific person should be appointed to do this. Demographic factors such as population, ethnicity, housing, health, education, employment and local economy should be taken into account. The needs of the local people often provide opportunities for church planters to give practical help as a prelude to sharing the gospel. For example, in Africa, missions often opened

---

[75] Stetzer, *Planting Missional Churches*, p239.

schools and hospitals alongside churches. In times of famine they provided food and shelter. Today, organisations like Tearfund, a relief agency charity, continue to provide practical help. They help local churches to improve basic services, such as redressing the lack of water, sanitation and the prevalence of hunger.[76] This follows the example of Christ Himself who said to His disciples, 'You give them something to eat' (Mark 6:37).

Today, churches in Britain are providing services to immigrants, such as English classes and help with legal matters. Other churches are providing a meeting place for the lonely, advice for those in debt, and help for drug addicts and the poor and homeless. In doing so they are following the example of Jesus, as recorded in the Gospels: 'When Jesus … saw a large crowd, he had compassion on them, because they were like sheep without a shepherd' (Mark 6:34, NIV UK).

The Bible shows us that God is concerned for people's bodies as well as their souls. Robinson and Smith note that:

> The central purpose of God to know Him personally has remained unchanged since the beginning of time and will remain unchanged until the end of time. Along the way, God has other concerns. He is concerned for the poor, for the weak and for the helpless. He is a God of justice.[77]

---

[76] More information about Tearfund is available at www.tearfund.org (accessed 23rd June 2017).

[77] Robinson and Smith, *Invading Secular Space*, p100.

Achieving critical mass

Opinions differ about the number of people needed to start a church. Peter Wagner stated in 1992 that it is advisable to have a group of at least fifty people before launching a new church.[78] This may not always be necessary. For example, when I came to the UK in December 2002, I started a church (Emmanuel Christian Fellowship UK Cities) with just two people. Now we have churches in two cities with a total of more than 100 members. Also, I have known some emergent host culture churches which were started just by a couple of people and grew quickly. Similarly, a multi-ethnic church can be started as a mission point in a house by a visionary leader and its core group.

However, as the church develops it must have a large enough team to do all the necessary jobs, such as preaching, leading services, music, children's work, ushering and serving refreshments, evangelism, secretarial and financial skills, pastoral gifts and practical skills such as IT. If the church doesn't have enough of all these gifts, it should be prepared to seek support from a congregation in its network. Where this happens, it is important that the loaned person contributes the specific skills that are absent from the group. But it is always preferable, rather than bringing the gifts in from outside, to develop the gifts of those in the planting team through specific training.

---

[78] Robinson Martin and Springs David, *Church Planting: The Training Manual* (Oxford: Lynx Communications, 1995), p127.

Reflection

- *How important is a) imagination and b) the work of the Holy Spirit in forming teams for strategic multi-cultural church planting? Describe a scenario where you could see these two elements coming together to achieve a successful church plant in your area or region.*

- *How important is research and strategic planning in establishing your multi-ethnic church plant? Enumerate the factors you need to be aware of before embarking on a new church plant in your area, and list the steps you would need to take in order to discover both needs and opportunities.*

Part Three

Reverse Mission

Reverse mission may also be known as 'incoming mission' or 'reverse flow mission'. The term is used to refer to the re-Christianising or re-evangelising of the West by former mission-receiving nations. Christians from nations formerly reached by Western missionaries are coming in large numbers to Western Europe to seek to bring the Christian faith back.

In this section we consider issues facing first-generation missionaries to the West, and in particular the challenges of the adjustments required to be made by their children. Many of the challenges they face are common to immigrants seeking to settle in a new culture, but they carry with them additional pressures arising from the nature of their role as missionaries within and to the host culture.

It can be observed that there are two kinds of first-generation missionaries in the West: those who came as economic or political refugees and then became unintentional missionaries, in that this had not been their primary goal, and those who travelled to the West as intentional missionaries. In previous sections of this book, we have seen that some migrants actively form churches which then become missional in character, though they did not come here with that intention but unwittingly became church planters. This process is distinct from that of intentional missionaries who came here specifically to plant churches with a view to reaching the host community for Christ. In the latter case, outreach to the indigenous population is a major focus from the outset, and this governs the missionary's relationship with the host culture in a different way from that of unintentional missionaries. This is not to say that unintentional missionaries are any less valuable, just that the route to their eventual calling is different, and this has consequences for their relationship with the host culture.

In what follows we will begin by surveying some of the challenges of acculturation facing reverse missionaries whichever way they came to that vocation, and we will go on to examine the particular challenges faced by their children, who form a separate subculture with their own distinct needs. In the process, we will attempt to assess the unique opportunities as well as challenges experienced by second-generation missionaries.

Chapter Six

First-generation Reverse Missionaries

We observed earlier that there are two types of first-generation reverse missionaries. The first are those who have come intentionally to reach the host culture with the gospel. The reasons for this will vary, either because they feel that they owe a debt to the society which first sent missionaries to evangelise their own nations, or because they see that the West has departed from its Christian heritage and is in need of rescue. The second group of missionaries have come as migrants to the West for other reasons and found themselves cast in the role of church leaders to their own ethnic group. They tend to become missionaries to the host culture as a second order activity after reflection on their position within the host culture. This places the two types of first-generation reverse missionaries in slightly different positions in relation to acculturation and attitudes to their calling and consequently to the host culture. Nevertheless, both groups of reverse missionaries need to accommodate to a second culture different from their own.

The range of reverse missionaries in the West is very diverse. I can think of Nigerian, Kenyan, Ethiopian, Polish and Romanian church planters, among others, who have a desire to engage in reverse mission. Beyond these, there are

South Koreans, Chinese, Brazilians, Peruvians and a sprinkling of Indians, as well as many francophone and anglophone Africans from a wide variety of nations.[79] This means that the first cultures from which these missionaries originate are widely diverse, and therefore the cultural accommodations that they make are also broadly different. This extends to the view of church that they bring to the missionary task as well as to cultural expectations of family life. Nevertheless, there are commonalities between the groups that we should consider.

Challenges reverse missionaries face

Acculturation

The key task, as most reverse missionaries see it, is for Western peoples to be converted. However, as they come to engage with Western culture they often discover that conversion is a much more complex task than they had expected. It entails the very real challenge of postmodernity – the loss of a belief in the possibility of finding a universal truth – which defines the world Westerners inhabit. In other words, the task of mission has to start much further back than the simple act of preaching the gospel, which is often treated with suspicion when Western people are confronted with it. Reverse missionaries have a passion to share the gospel, but soon discover they need to learn about their new host culture in

---

[79] See Hugh Osgood, 'The Rise of Black Churches' in David Goodhew, ed, *Church Growth in Britain 1980 to the Present* (Farnham: Ashgate Publishing, 2010), p109 for details.

order to be able to acculturate both themselves and their message.

One important lesson reverse missionaries are learning is that most Western late-modern people need to form friendships and relationships with believers long before they will show signs of any interest in their faith. This can be a hard lesson for reverse missionaries to learn, many of whom are used to cultures where the gospel can be quickly shared, but it is a necessary one if they are to make a meaningful impact on Western people with the claims of Christ and the gospel of salvation.

Language learning

In my experience, a real challenge to doing reverse mission was learning to speak the host country's language. I am not the only one who has faced this challenge – most of the first generation of oversees missionaries in the UK who do not have English as their mother tongue encounter the same problem.

Often, first-generation migrant churches engage in worship in their homeland language. Yet inviting a Westerner to a service that does not worship in English is a barrier to missionary engagement and relationship building. Reverse missionaries will do much better if they are part of a multi-ethnic church where English is the main language; they will learn to speak English more quickly and it will provide a community to which the reverse missionary can bring faith seekers.

Supporting themselves

Being a reverse missionary is often a significant sacrifice. In my case, when I was first planting churches in Europe, I would engage in the missionary work as well my usual paid work that funded it. During the first few years I worked in a factory so that I could earn the money to study and obtain an accountancy qualification. I also engaged in mission during this time. Then I decided to do an MA in Missional Leadership at the same time as engaging in church planting, paying for all of this through accountancy work. This MA proved very important to prepare me to effectively think through how to engage in reverse mission in a contextually relevant manner.

Other reverse missionaries known to me engage in mission and church planting during the day and then work nights to support their ministries and their families. Some of my students at ForMission College work night shifts to support their mission and their study during the day. It must be emphasised there is often not a sending church that pays the reverse missionary's salary. It is the sense of call and passion that God has put in such a person's heart that sustains the mission endeavour. In this sense, it would seem obvious that this kind of ministry is not entered into lightly, but it is based on a deep conviction that this is the purpose of God based on His love for the world.

Isolation

A real issue of concern is that many reverse missionaries can feel isolated, alone and left to fend for themselves, with the deep knowledge that many people do not understand their specific challenges. For example, some of my students face challenges over their study, supporting their families and engaging in their ministries, which simply cannot be easily appreciated by Westerners unless they take the time to get to know them better. What has helped me and my students has been when tutors and colleagues have offered support that can make the difference between success or at times failure or greater hardship. I know that those of us who are achieving the dreams God has put in our hearts are deeply grateful to Western professionals and Christian leaders for the support they provide. For example, this book would not be possible if it were not for colleagues that have offered helpful suggestions and editorial comments.

All students can face difficulties, but in my experience of teaching reverse missionary students and Westernised missional students, the challenges faced by the former are often of a different order to those faced by the latter. The table below details a brief overview of the key challenges my students face.

Key challenges of reverse missionary students vs host culture students

Student category	Profile	Issues	Strengths/ advantages	Challenges/ weaknesses
Immigrant students (African and others)	Mostly pastors Mostly parents Workers Passionate about ministry Age 45-60 English as second or other language	Been out of formal education for years Unfamiliar with Western education Slow in comprehension Expectation/ idea of a Christian college Unfamiliar with technology No family support structure Emergency, family-related long distance travel Home environment not suitable for individual study Time constraints for individual study	Persistent effort and hard-working Motivated for mission and actually engaged in placements	May not respond to emails Time management Likely to 'suffer in silence' in the face of allegations, eg suspected plagiarism, because of respect for authority Traditionalist – limited academic style Shame-based handling of certain issues Not easy to access financial support, eg student loan Some discriminatory practices

Student category	Profile	Issues	Strengths/ advantages	Challenges/ weaknesses
Home students (White British)	English as first language Generally Western education background Not much church leadership role Some parents New to ministry (Exploring ministry opportunities) Some young, middle-aged & older Supportive family structure	Hesitation in accessing student support resulting in being easily neglected when support is being offered Little or no ministry experience Quitting or withdrawing from course easily done	Stronger academic competence Quick learners Confidently disclose any disability Has individual or personal reading/study time at home Easier access to public funds/ work/resources	Easily give up Self-doubt

How some of these reverse missionary challenges can be overcome

Learning a host culture's language

There are numerous routes open to learn the language. In the UK, some will go to English as a Second Language classes with a view to passing an appropriate course. My students who are learning about reverse mission are given English support and also take part in English classes. Of course, the best way to learn a language is to challenge oneself by speaking English on an everyday basis. In other words, practice makes perfect, whether it be through reading, writing, listening or speaking.

Means to understand the host culture

The path to accommodating oneself with the host culture is not a simple one – but speaking the language makes it far easier! Most reverse missionaries will have at least a basic working knowledge of the dominant language of the host culture. In order to become effective missionaries, they will need to improve on this but, as we have seen, evangelistic and pastoral concerns in their initial church plant can mitigate against progress. Many reverse missionaries struggle with this and only a few enrol for language school to hone their skills.

However, language skills are not the only priority; there is also the question of acquiring an adequate working knowledge and understanding of the world view of the host culture and the way in which the society operates. This is not a simple matter, yet a great deal hinges upon it in terms of effectiveness. There are many cultural traps to be avoided as well as skills to be taken on board to become adept at relating to the indigenous population. It takes a great deal of adaptive skill to negotiate change from a communal culture to a predominantly individualistic ethos, and whatever skills are acquired, there is no substitute for living within the diverse host culture as opposed to remaining within the originating monoculture of the initial church plant. Many reverse missionaries find it difficult to adjust to a culture with a different attitude to truth-telling, for instance. Many of them come from honour–shame based cultures, where the opinion of the group is more important than messages from an inbuilt conscience as a guide to truth-telling – that is more characteristic of a Western guilt-based culture. Part of the transition into the values of the host culture will include that of negotiating the educational process for the missionary's children, who may be key to the process of bridging the cultural gap in the longer term.

The reverse missionary is also forced to contend with domestic pressures, not least of which is maintaining a bridge between their own culture and that of the host culture to which any children will already be exposed through school and the media. The missionary's spouse may be a frontline member of the missionary team or a domestic or financial support for their own mission activity. In either case, there will be domestic pressures created by living between two diverse cultures. Often, child-rearing will be part of this process, which makes its own demands, while at the same time providing opportunities for contact with the host culture via medical, educational and welfare support systems.

An additional component of the acculturation process that frequently comes into play is that of financial support. Reverse missionaries rarely enjoy the luxury of financial support from sending churches and, even where they do, the exchange rate usually devalues the external contributions that they may receive. Indeed, many reverse missionaries do not come from a sending church; many of them are entrepreneurial. Thus, the missionary either resorts to secular employment to help finance their outreach work, or seeks recourse to the ethnic minority church plant to finance their mission activity. Either of these sources of income places strains on the missionary endeavour, in the former case in terms of diverted time and energy, and in the latter, in terms of the new congregation's expectations for the missionary's primary activity. It is worth noting that African missionaries are more likely to be entrepreneurs[80] while Koreans, at the other end of the scale, are almost always sent by a parent church. This may be in part because many South Korean missionaries come from large Presbyterian or Methodist church structures that are more corporate in their approach. Moreover, South Korea is a relatively wealthy nation, so able to support their more extensive work around the globe financially.

Other opportunities and challenges

The bulk of reverse mission takes place in metropolitan areas; the target for such mission activity is usually large cities or major industrial towns, simply because this is where most immigrants from their home cultures are to be found, and this is the obvious starting point for planting churches that will eventually reach out to the host culture. It is manifestly easier to begin the work of mission within one's own language group and culture.

---

[80] A Olo Matthes, 'Reverse Mission' in Jonathan J Bonk, *The Routledge Encyclopedia of Missions and Missionaries* (Abingdon: Routledge, 2010), pp380-382.

The missionary will normally find it relatively easy to gather people from their own cultural group, some of whom may already be Christians, to incorporate and thus to establish a worshipping community. This has advantages, since people from the missionary's culture will be looking for some kind of social anchor, and the attraction of associating with people who share language, dress and food preferences is an obvious gathering point. The disadvantage in terms of reaching the host culture is that to facilitate this gathering together, worship will tend to be in the language and cultural norms of the minority ethnic culture, and thus forms a barrier to touching the lives of the host community. This is a barrier which needs to be broken down in the next generation if mission is to be accomplished, and in this respect, missionary children stand in a unique position since they understand both their parents' culture and the host culture. As was discussed earlier, they form a third culture, drawing on both of these, and have been designated by sociologists as 'third-culture children'.

However, discipling these children can be difficult, and this can be illustrated in the following way. The reverse missionary comes from a particular culture and is hence a monocultural person. Although they are a people from a monocultural background, they find themselves serving in a muted or semi-multicultural and multinational community. The challenge, then, is that the missionary emphasises their originating monoculture to the detriment of an emergent multicultural and multinational setting. The missionary identifies only with the understanding of a single background with the same skin colour, language and shared values. However, this is not true of their children. In this setting, third-culture children experience alienation and consequently disconnect from their family and missional community. Further, they find it difficult to join other faith groups because they fear this would bring shame to their family. Consequently, they are likely to be overtaken by secularism, thus becoming part of the problem rather than part of the solution.

One of the dangers of this typical monocultural approach to the task of reverse mission is that the church planter quickly becomes pastor to the new church and then pastoral issues tend to take up the bulk of their time and effort, thereby diverting energy from the task of mission itself. Another unintended consequence is that for the most part, this pastoral activity is bound to be conducted in the missionary's native language, thus delaying the language acquisition skills needed to reach the host community effectively. This brings us full circle, back to the attractive option for reverse missionaries to either plant a multi-ethnic or multicultural congregation. As I mentioned earlier, this is one way that language issues could be addressed not just for the leader but also for their monocultural church. Clearly it might take time to transition a monocultural church to partner with a congregation made up of another culture, but it is a real possibility that needs to be considered.

Reflection

- *As a reverse missionary church leader, how do you plan to avoid spending most of your time caring for your own community?*

- *What steps are you taking to improve your English language skills?*

- *How do you propose to refocus your own community on mission to the host community?*

Forming multicultural churches

Plainly, the trick for reverse missionaries is to form missional churches right from the outset, but this is easier said than done. What is required is a new generation of reverse missionaries who are equipped to understand what missional church entails, and who are given the tools to make this possible. It is desirable to get ahead of the curve by equipping reverse missionaries either at source or over here before they begin the task. The successful reverse missionary, if they are truly to reach the host culture, should begin by planting an initial church, whether from their own people group or from the host culture, which understands that mission is the lifeblood of the church and the engine of evangelisation in the host culture. There needs to be a fuller appreciation of what it means for the church to be missional, with the result that mission becomes its DNA.

Parallels with nineteenth-century Western missionaries

Reverse mission can be traced back to the period of Western missionaries to Africa and other mission fields. In my mind, I look back to the early beginnings of mission, its background, the oral stories I have heard from my fellow countrymen, and recently, reading the missiologist Harvey Kwiyani's personal narrative about Western missionaries in his village when he was growing up as a young boy. His story refers to the missionaries' graves, and he identifies the sacrifices they made.

There are some hard truths to be understood from the first phase of first-generation missionaries. They faced stiff challenges, often in the shape of financial hardship, unstable family settings, difficulties bringing up their children, and, of course, challenges arising out of situations in which familiar support structures were no longer available as they came to terms with living in a new and different culture. This caused me to pause and reflect, as a reverse missionary in Europe, that mission in general requires sacrifice, and reverse mission likewise demands sacrifices. It would be folly to think of genuine reverse missionaries as living a life of pleasure, enjoying Western wealth!

Given all these costs, it can be worth wondering who would want to follow in their footsteps. But perhaps this is when they reap some benefit in their children, given that the missionaries' offspring may be among those who will become the most effective missionaries of the future generation owing to their being more fully acculturated than their parents.

Chapter Seven

The Second Generation: Children of First-generation Missionaries

Sociologists examining the phenomenon of immigrant children, children of military and foreign service personnel and missionary children have labelled them as 'third-culture children' or as 'missionary kids'. What they share is that they come from one culture, settle in another and as a subgroup form a distinct culture of their own – the so-called 'third culture'.

We will focus on the children of first-generation missionaries who form a unique example of third-culture children. The sociologists Pollock and Van Reken comment:

> A Third Culture Kid (TCK) is a person who has spent a significant part of his or her development years outside their parents' culture. The TCK builds relationships to all the cultures, while not having full ownership in any. Although elements from each culture are assimilated into the TCK's

life experience, the sense of belonging is in relationship to others of a similar background.[81]

Pollock and Van Reken point out that these children display a number of common attributes that make both them and their situation unique. These characteristics impact their relationship with their parents' founding church and pose problems as well as opportunities for mission. These authors suggest that rootlessness and restlessness often characterise third-culture children. [82] This is because they have little sense of belonging either to their parents' culture or to that which they have adopted. At the same time, they display tendencies in later life always to want to move on to a different location or setting. There is a strong tendency for these children to develop only superficial relationships within the host culture, finding instead their most significant bonds with people like themselves who form part of a third culture that is neither that of their parents' nor of the host culture.

The challenge for reverse mission is to find ways of anchoring these children firmly in the host culture while enabling them to retain their attachments to their parental culture. Part of this challenge rests with the way their home congregation negotiates the transition from monocultural forms of worship and communication to forms that are amenable to the host culture. So far in this country there are few signs of reverse mission congregations that have

---

[81] D C Pollock and R E Van Reken, *Third Culture Kids: The Experience of Growing Up Among Worlds* (London: Nicholas Brealey Publishing, 2009), p19.

[82] Pollock and Van Reken, *Third Culture Kids*, p123ff.

achieved this. The few exceptions are large African congregations that began by reaching out to migrants from a variety of different African countries, thus forcing them to adopt English as the common means of communication and worship, since congregants came from former British colonies where English was widely spoken.

Challenges and adjustments for third-culture children

Pollock and Van Reken refer to what anthropologist Gary Weaver calls 'the cultural iceberg'. The part of an iceberg visible to the naked eye is a small part of its structure; the bulk of it lies unseen below the waterline. Pollock and Van Reken comment:

> The part above the water can be considered *surface culture* – what we can physically see or hear, including behaviour, words, customs, language and traditions. Underneath the water, invisible to all, is the *deep culture*. This place includes our beliefs, values, assumptions, worldview and thought processes.[83]

It is this deep culture, which is imparted in the context of the home, that marks out third-culture children as different. The reason for this is because what has been encoded into them in their homes is often perceived to be at odds with the surface culture of the host culture they are growing up in. The question of culture is so vexing for

---

[83] Pollock and Van Reken, *Third Culture Kids*, p42.

some that it needs to be seriously engaged with in multicultural communities. Young people are beginning to experience an alternative set of social values, and these are often different from what they see played out within the home setting. In homes where there are strong patriarchal practices, for example, third-culture girls often become hostile to such practices, seeing them as unfair and out of keeping with their experiences in the host culture. They may additionally experience some negative practices from the host culture which adds to their rootlessness. One example would be the lack of respect for elders in Western culture compared to many homeland cultures that their parents originate from.

Outwardly, third-culture children may learn to conform to the host culture in terms of visible appearance and increasingly of language, but they carry around with them a mixed set of values. This means that these children do not feel that they fully fit either their parents' culture or the host culture in which they are being brought up,[84] and as a result can lack an adequate cultural identity model. [85] Because these children do not share the same identity as their parents, they experience a hidden diversity which enables them to negotiate cultural variety, although this may be at the cost of a loss or exchange of role models and what Pollock and Van Reken describe as a lack of 'system identity'.[86] This can give rise to confused loyalties which their parents may either be unaware of or strive to avoid

---

[84] Pollock and Van Reken, *Third Culture Kids*, p54.

[85] Pollock and Van Reken, *Third Culture Kids*, p55.

[86] Pollock and Van Reken, *Third Culture Kids*, p79.

by cocooning them within the first church structures and its cultural certainties.

The experience of third-culture children is not all one of loss – they may also enjoy the benefits of cross-cultural enrichment, an expanded world view and expanded relationships.[87] However, it is frequently true that such children find their main terms of reference within their own third culture, consisting of other children with a similar background or from the church to which they belong.

Nevertheless, as third-culture children grow up, they tend to conform more and more to the host culture in terms of language and surface customs. This means the worship and medium of communication that they encounter in their parents' church become more and more alien to them. Many reverse missionaries decide at this point that their church plant needs to transition from its native language to that of the host culture so as to retain the loyalty and commitment of their own children. They also see this as a means of reaching out to the indigenous culture. However, many of their church members, especially those without children, tend to resist such moves, since the existing church culture confirms them in their own ethnic and cultural identity. This causes real tension between the needs of the existing congregation, the needs of the emerging congregation of the next generation, and the task of evangelism in the host culture.

The only way that this tendency can be successfully combated is by ensuring that from the outset of its

---

[87] Pollock and Van Reken, *Third Culture Kids*, pp 90-96.

formation the congregation is focused on its missionary task. If this is done and the children of the congregation are brought up with the recognition that they are a vital part of this task, then third-culture children are well placed to fulfil their unique role in making reverse mission a success.

Reflection

- *What part do children within your own congregation play in terms of furthering the task of reverse mission?*

- *How should you structure the worship and teaching in your congregation to ensure a smooth transition into the host culture for the children of church members?*

Retaining third-generation children

Third-culture children may well be a vital factor in the success of the work of reverse mission, but how are they to be retained so as to become that vital part of this undertaking? Little serious work has been done in this area to date, and some considered strategy needs to be put in place. Many reverse missionaries suggest that the way forward is to recruit indigenous youth and children's workers in their churches to become partners in mission with a dedicated responsibility of easing their children and young people into a frontline role in reaching the host culture. This is a definite possibility, and such a move would have the added benefit of making mission a truly cross-cultural enterprise. It would also provide alternative role models for reverse mission young people as they grow up.

One way in which third-culture children may be acculturated into a truly multicultural, multi-ethnic church experience might not only be by employing indigenous children's and youth workers, but also by forming partnerships with youth groups in existing host-cultural churches so that their disciple-making takes place in a multicultural context. This could have the added benefit of raising the awareness of the indigenous partner churches. The issue becomes one of structuring churches on both sides of the fence in such a way that they foster a multicultural experience of church and discipleship. Both sides would need to understand that each one of them has something both to give to and to learn from their partners in the gospel.

The challenges facing third-culture children are real. Once my son, who was just starting nursery school in Leeds, asked me, 'Dad, where do I come from? Where is home?' My friend's son in an early years school setting asked him, 'What is my name in Zambia?' Still another little girl asked her mother, 'Why are most of the people who come home black?' All these questions, and many more like them, are concerned with the idea of home, family, relationships and identity. They underline the question and sense of belonging, the quest to fit in, but also puzzling with experiences of dos and don'ts and difference. In developing multicultural communities, third-culture children ought to find resolutions to these questions. The multicultural community which is developed or established on strong biblical tenets should become the home in which third-culture children find confidence in their 'belongingness' within the household of God, the space to realise their dreams, and the passion to seek and respond to difference competently. In other words, the multicultural community is the level playing ground where the gospel can be the ultimate filter through which competing or cultural tensions can be harmonised.

There are other factors that advance the reality of the multicultural community – for example, the dynamic of globalisation evident in the light of advancements in how youth culture is communicated all over the world, through music, fashion, TV, films, etc. Gone is the time when a young person in the UK was influenced by different popular culture expectations compared to a youth in Asia or South America. Globalisation has created an expectation that young people have similar rights to become their own self-determining persons. Third-culture children are already very good at this, and so they often do not have the inhibitions and prejudices about interacting on the world stage that other cultures or people groups may have. This means that third-culture children are already primed by globalisation for membership into the multicultural community.

Another factor to bear in mind is the birth rate. The UK population is ageing, so the country must depend on the migrant communities to support the nation. However, migrant communities cannot look to themselves as the only panacea to save the declining indigenous British population. This would be to deny the richness of British culture, which third-culture children are adopting for their own survival and, by extension, the survival of the Church.

In their free interactions with their peers from the host communities, third-culture children are learning and adapting to the niceties of British culture, norms and traditions, and appreciating their values in ways closed to previous generations. The inevitability of the development of multicultural communities means that third-culture children, who are an increasing part of the population, already possess the necessary world view essential for the mission of God. Third-culture children need, therefore, to be considered as the new elect necessary for churches to be planted as multi-ethnic communities for mission.

Tapping their potential

If these suggestions are taken seriously, it is clear that third-culture children could have a vital part to play in reverse mission. Third-culture children and young people represent an enormous potential to be tapped in forming bridges into the host culture. For this to happen, it is necessary to prepare and equip them from their earliest days to become partners in mission with their parents.

I know of one case where a church-planting couple in this country taught their two children from the outset that they were partners in their mission, and encouraged them to mix with and reach out to their peers in school and to invite them to their home. As he grew up, the son went on to found and lead an effective Christian Union in his high school and to help build a nascent youth church led by his parents. He is now at a Christian university in the United States reading theology and will go on to take a Master's degree in Missions in preparation for becoming a missionary himself. The younger daughter quietly witnessed in school and led other girls to Christ. An accomplished musician, her ambition is to graduate as a teacher and become a music therapist working with educationally disadvantaged children. Mission takes many different forms, and it is important for third-culture children to grow up realising they are privileged with a unique life trajectory which equips them not only for mission, but also for life in a multicultural world.

To conclude this section, although third-culture children may find it hard to negotiate their identity in society, they also develop special strengths. Among these is emotional intelligence, and the ability to more consciously recognise cultural differences in others and negotiate their relationships interculturally better as a result. Moreover, in my experience, it is worth bearing in mind that the reverse missionary parents of third-culture children may gain an audience with the host culture because they offer a whole new world view, in spirituality, passion, language, intellect and energy. Such differences may invite the curious to seek answers outside their belief framework. Today, the newer, second-generation reverse missionaries are emerging and bringing to mission a new set of skills, experiences, ideas and ways of engaging in mission that is distinct from the first generation, which they have learned from their parents' experiences where their cultural difference has attracted people in the host culture's interest. Their parents forged the way ahead by trying to acculturate in a host culture because of their difference to it. This new wave is not content with operating only within their own cultural group, but instead are developing new competencies which will bridge the gap between themselves and the host culture. Theirs is an even more rigorous approach to the development of multi-ethnic communities and leadership which contemporary society clearly needs.

Reflection/Action

- *How can third-culture children become an asset in pursuit of mission to the host culture?*
- *Formulate a long-term plan for transitioning into a multicultural missional community.*

Part Four

Mentoring

Chapter Eight

Mentoring for African Missional Leaders

This case study might help us understand some of the principles leading to the establishment and growth of multi-ethnic churches in Europe. It is drawn from personal experience with developing and mentoring leaders in African Christian communities in the UK, which might help us formulate a template which could be adapted to fit other circumstances.

On first coming to the UK as an intentional reverse missionary, I faced unanticipated issues and in the process made some mistakes that could have been avoided if only someone had come alongside me to point the way. Most reverse missionaries from the African diaspora today do not arrive with the intention of engaging in reverse mission, therefore their need for guidance when they find themselves in the role is even greater. The popular writer Israel Olofinjana in his book, *Turning the Tables on Mission*,[88] identifies case examples of those like myself who face the challenges of reverse mission in the Western context.

---

[88] I Olofinjana, *Turning the Tables on Mission: Stories of Christians from the global south in the UK* (Watford: Instant Apostle, 2013).

To begin with, I was full of passion based on the vision God had given to me, and I was keen to become a prolific church planter, so I spread myself too thinly, seeking to plant churches in London, Leicester, Bradford and Leeds, all at the same time! It quickly became apparent that a better plan would be to localise, so we moved to Leeds where we planted an Amharic-speaking church. To become more effective in reaching the host community – which was always my main objective – I enrolled for an MA in Missional Leadership. It was from there that recognition grew that the most effective way both to plant ethnic churches and to reach out to the indigenous population would be to train leaders to multiply our reach.

The truth is that while training leaders is always a good thing, leaders are born by calling, gifting and mentoring. Thus, classroom training is not sufficient; indeed, head knowledge on its own can go disastrously wrong. Experience is a great teacher, and tempers head knowledge with a good dose of practical reality. Mentoring is not a new process; the issue is not 'Should it be done?' as much as 'Should it be done well or merely haphazardly?'

For reverse missionaries, some mentors might be found among people of their own culture who have learned about crossing cultural boundaries for the sake of mission. But I would also suggest that other mentors will need to be found from the host culture, people who can give rich insights into the world the reverse missionary is seeking to reach.

The African diaspora in Europe has grown exponentially. Many of the newcomers to these shores did not come with the intention of becoming missionaries to the host culture, but they were passionate Christians to whom it quickly became apparent that the European culture that they once thought of as Christian now itself needed to be redeemed. This led many of them first to found migrant or expatriate churches and then to seek to reach out to the wider culture. The opportunities are immense; however, the road to becoming reverse missionaries is full of dead ends and roadblocks. Many of these could be avoided with the help and guidance of those who have trodden the way before them, hence the need for intentional mentoring.

Since 2003, when I started ministry in the UK, under the guidance of the Holy Spirit I first planted Amharic-speaking churches and, through a series of events, established a wider network of African leaders. This helped me to see that we are all reverse missionaries, working from a diaspora base, and we face many of the same issues. At this time, my existing burden from God to train missional leaders caused me to start the Leeds learning centre of Springdale College, which is today known as ForMission College Leeds campus, which helped me to discern in greater detail what the needs of African diaspora church leaders were. This, in turn, provided the impulse to write this part of the book, in order to fill the gap in literature that addresses the need for new ways of engaging in intercultural leadership, and additionally to make each church planter and missionary more effective in redoubling their efforts to plant self-reproducing communities of faith. To put it simply, we have discovered that enthusiasm on its own is not enough.

As I pen this on a writing retreat in the south of Portugal, I have been watching a mother stork on her nest on the chimney tops. Returning from a fishing expedition with a full belly, she regurgitates her catch to feed her young. Later, she will be teaching them to fish for themselves, since she knows the goal is to set them free to establish their own families, thus re-establishing the cycle all over again. There is a lesson to be learned from this example of the stork, and it is one that both Jesus and the apostle Paul knew well, since mentoring was the basic pattern for the duplicative discipleship pattern that they practised.

We see this same potential in African leaders, but instinct alone will not do; we need to take steps to make sure that duplication in the next generation is built into the DNA of mission from the beginning. Recent research has come up with an unexpected finding. University of Cambridge scientists have found that when the human genome is damaged by starvation or trauma, the distorted gene can be passed on to succeeding generations. There is need to heed this lesson. Faulty leadership will lead to malnourished or deformed churches, and the process of mission itself may be brought to a halt. When it comes to mission, it behoves us to get it right for the sake of God's kingdom. It is not that mentors have all the answers, but at least there is a place for seasoned veterans to help the next generation of leaders to get it right in their own context.

The African diaspora church experience has tended to be monocultural. But to develop into multi-ethnic communities for mission, the mentoring relationship needs to be adopted as a tool for equipping new leaders. As a starting point, the immediate task is to understand what the term 'mentoring' means.

Reflection

- *Name the three most influential people in your life up to this point.*
- *How did they influence you?*
- *Was their influence intentional or accidental?*
- *How did you make the most of these relationships?*

What is mentoring?

There are many definitions of mentoring, most of which suggest a particular theme or area of influence where the mentoring is in use. In this book, the focus is on Christian mentoring, although the core elements are likely to exist in other forms of mentoring outside the Church. The writer John Mallison defines Christian mentoring as 'a dynamic, intentional relationship of trust in which one person enables another to maximize the grace of God in their life and service'. [89] In ministry, different individuals are endowed with gifts or talents and each person is obliged to use these talents for the whole Church to be effective.[90] As

---

[89] John Mallison, *Mentoring: To Develop Disciples & Leaders* (Australia: Scripture Union and Open Book Publishers, 1998), p8.

[90] Carson Pue, *Mentoring Leaders Wisdom for Developing, Calling, and Competency* (Grand Rapids, MI: Baker Books, 2005), p97.

John Maxwell says, people tend to become what the most important person in their lives thinks they will become, while Rick Warren observes that the Church can be a creative space for all sorts of talents. [91] In Mallison's definition, these talents are seen as gifts of grace such that the abundance or fullness of grace can be reached or maximised in a mentoring relationship. Mallison describes this mentoring process as 'dynamic' and 'intentional', indicating that it is neither static nor accidental, but alive, changing and deliberate. Further, a vital ingredient in mentoring is trust, without which mentoring is likely to break down. Another definition is given by the mentoring thinker Gunter Krallmann:

> A mentor in the Biblical sense establishes a close relationship with a protégé and on that basis through fellowship, modeling, advice, encouragement, correction, practical assistance and prayer support influences his/her understudy to gain a deeper comprehension of divine truth, lead a godlier life and render more effective service to God.[92]

In this definition, mentoring focuses on a number of activities, such as information-giving and guidance. Mallison speaks of maximising grace, whereas Krallman

---

[91] John C Maxwell, *Developing the Leaders Within You* (Nashville, TN: Thomas Nelson Publishers, 1993), p116; Rick Warren, *The Purpose Driven Church*, p312.

[92] Gunter Krallmann, *Mentoring for Mission* (Hong Kong: Jensco Ltd and Germany: Globe Europe, 1992), p122.

indicates the purpose of mentoring as leading ultimately to God. They indicate that the mentor is the senior friend or fellow who is also a guide or model who helps the mentee to become more godly. The mentee or protégé is an understudy, almost suggestive of an apprentice or potential successor.

Rick Lewis, in his book *Mentoring Matters*, after a careful analysis of various definitions, opts for the following expression:

> Within intentional, empowering, unique relationships, Christian mentoring identifies and promotes the work of God's Spirit in others' lives, assisting them to access God's resources for their growth and strength in spirituality, character and ministry.[93]

Some of the characteristics in Lewis' definition have already been suggested by Krallman and Mallison. Without repeating those definitions, it is worth highlighting some key features from the mentoring expert Lewis' description. Firstly, mentoring varies from one relationship to another. It is a unique relationship; it does not produce a copy of the mentor. Secondly, it is about knowing and responding to the Holy Spirit in people's lives. Thirdly, it is about character-building, empowering, and leading to maturity or growth, spiritually and otherwise.

---

[93] Rick Lewis, *Mentoring Matters* (Oxford, MI: Monarch Books, 2009), p20.

What is lacking in the above definition is not so much what mentoring is, but that the mentor is cast in the role of a rather clever detective seeking out what the Holy Spirit is doing and being the channel through which God brings it about. However, drawing upon Lewis' definition, for African diaspora missional contexts, this book describes mentoring as helping potential leaders to develop character, spirituality and ministry capacities. Bearing in mind the missional context, an important part of this book is to provide an understanding for African diaspora churches. My working definition has been chosen because it not only embraces the various definitions discussed by Lewis and others, but also captures the aspirations of African diaspora church leaders and reverse missionaries seeking to develop multicultural communities for mission in a new cultural context.

My working definition of mentoring is, 'the process of realising and releasing potential in the mentee, through guidance reflection and correction'. This is virtually a definition of the New Testament term 'exhortation': we know that people are born with certain natural talents and some with a special gift of serving God through offering service to people (see 1 Corinthians 12:4). In Genesis 5:29 Noah was given a name which means 'comfort', since, 'Out of the ground that the Lord has cursed this one shall bring us relief from our work and from the painful toil of our hands.' Thus, he was called to be the means of redeeming the gifts and talents distorted by man's rebellion. Those who are born again are additionally endowed with spiritual gifts with which to serve God, not just for their own enjoyment. These gifts, however, can be enhanced or developed under the guidance of a mentor.

Reflection

- *Which definition of mentoring is most helpful to you?*
- *Do you think you might benefit from such a relationship?*
- *How might you perform this function for someone else in a ministry relationship to you?*

The value of mentoring

Most African church leaders have talent, potential and vision in abundance, but the problems come when they try to transplant previous experience of church growth, church planting and evangelism acquired from their African roots into European soil. They quickly find that the equation is not so simple, and so they either become discouraged or they regress into concentrating all their efforts on creating and maintaining expatriate churches on European soil. This is where the value of mentoring from an experienced intercultural practitioner can help them to understand the host culture better. Experience is obviously the operative term in this case. The mentor will need a proven track record in successfully helping reverse missionaries to acculturate to a Western context, in order to be able to help them adjust and address the right issues.

African leaders come to the task of ministry with an innate spirituality and energy that can find full expression and satisfaction within their own monocultural churches. But is this what it means to be an effective missionary or church leader in the European context? More aware African diaspora church leaders will be dissatisfied with apparent numerical success within their own people group when they know that the biblical calling is to reach all nations with the gospel of Jesus Christ. They realise that their spiritual energy and enthusiasm is a gift from God and a vital cultural contribution that they have to make to the churches of the host community, yet they lack awareness of how to translate this into effective action.

It is clear that enthusiasm and a sense of calling are not sufficient on their own. What is needed is enabling and empowering input from people who have walked the way before them, who may be able to help them chart a way forward into fruitful and successful ministry that will truly impact the host environment. The problem is not so much a lack of skills to implement vision; it is, rather, a matter of discovering potential through character development – an important component in the tool box of ministry skills – and in the process acquiring wisdom in the exercise of ministry and the development of relationships.

Jesus, our example

Before going on to look at the nature of the mentoring process, it is worth thinking about the problems faced by all missionaries and church leaders entering another culture. These are the same ones that I – and others like me – faced when beginning ministry in the UK. In no particular order, these are issues of finance, orientation and understanding the host culture and what makes it tick.

None of these is easily resolved without guidance and help to overcome them in any given set of circumstances.

Remember, no two situations are exactly alike, and therefore there is no infallible 'how to' manual for missionary success; if there were, God would have handed it over to us when we received our calling. Instead, He chose to deliver the gospel incarnationally – that is, in embodied form – and, like Jesus, the supreme mentor, we have to make our way as we listen to the Father in dependence on the Holy Spirit. This does not mean that we don't need others who may be God's mouthpiece or signposts for us. On the contrary, as Krallman points out, even Jesus had to grow within His own Jewish culture under the guidance of godly parents to whom God had entrusted Him (Luke 2:51-52). Key to preparing even the Son of God in His human nature for the role of both Saviour and mentor was orientation within the culture to which He came. Why should it be any different for us?

Contemporary state of mentoring in missional context

If the Ethiopian and Eritrean churches in Yorkshire (UK) are taken as an example of what is happening with migrant churches in general, and African churches in particular, we can understand some of these mentoring dynamics in a real missional context. One form of group worship in Yorkshire had its origins in a small group of Ethiopians meeting together as friends and sharing prayers from time to time. The first structured church, Emmanuel Christian Fellowship, was formed in 2003 in Leeds. Currently, there are four churches in Leeds, four in Sheffield and one in Huddersfield.

This growth is encouraging, yet the enormity of the task is evident when compared with the overall Ethiopian and Eritrean population. Furthermore, this does not even take into account the wider societal context. Only three of these churches have more than fifty members. The implication for mission and leadership here is that there is a need to recognise the potential for greater growth, the need for a new crop of leaders, and the need to ensure that these leaders are properly equipped to expedite or facilitate growth. This is likely to be the case for other African diaspora churches in the UK. In order to meet these needs, mentoring will be the most effective tool to help these church leaders rise to the challenges likely to be met in mission.

There is, however, already within most African churches some form of mentoring taking place. It is my observation that this mentoring takes place in an informal way. There is no recognisable framework for mentoring arrangements, but there is a visible pattern in which mentoring occurs. The lack of an informed mentoring programme highlights the arbitrary nature of support that is currently available. Mentors assume their roles often without adequate training but with vast experience in ministry. Often, the mentor is, as it were, a patron, or sponsor, and may be referred to as 'my spiritual father', a title and role that is informal but becoming generally popular.

A criticism regarding mentoring can be if the mentee becomes a protégé of a mentor, which would be paternalistic if it were permitted to occur. Moreover, the idea of mentoring as lifelong is not reasonable. However, in the Ethiopian and Eritrean contexts, owing to their reputation and experience, the mentor often plays a role far beyond merely developing leadership. For example, in some situations the mentor may be called to act as judge, being invited to pass a decision on the basis that they are more experienced and they have the interests of their mentee at heart. Examples of these situations include conflict resolution between church members, or marriage problems.

In my view, there is need within African diaspora churches for a more regularised, harmonised and structured mentoring programme. It is my experience within the missional context that pastors, teachers and others in ministry are beginning to indicate value in having some form of arrangement in which they receive from their more experienced colleagues a shoulder to lean on at various stages of the mission journey.[94] This is not just on the pastor-to-pastor level, but also at the church-to-church level. For example, a 'mother church' or church-planting church, acts as mentor to a newly planted church, as is the case between Emmanuel Christian Fellowship in Leeds and Emmanuel Christian Fellowship in Sheffield. A mentoring model similar to this arrangement is the group mentoring model illustrated by Sanders, which carries the

---

[94] A pastor at Rhema Faith Ministry in Leeds has a mentoring relationship with London-based pastor Apostle Zewude, and a pastor at Emmanuel Christian Fellowship has found mentoring from Dr Richard Whitehouse very useful.

added benefit for groups of fostering learning among participants.[95]

Reflection

- *List the advantages and disadvantages of informal mentoring.*
- *How could a formal relationship with a trained mentor improve your performance?*

The importance of intentional mentoring

Taking into consideration the factors outlined above, current mentoring practices need to be identified, as it is clear that the use of mentoring as a means of developing new leaders is crucial for the growth of these churches. Mentoring would help new leaders to understand the needs of the church, and to make changes in their church or in planting new churches. Mentoring would also help them to avoid repeating the same mistakes, such as failing to have new leaders to take over, or avoiding divisions within the church, which the previous leadership may have created when planting new churches.

An important element of the mentoring relationship is to understand what is involved. It will not be possible in such a short space to do justice to this subject because of

---

[95] Martin Sanders, *The Power of Mentoring: Shaping People Who Will the World* (Camp Hill, PA: WingSpread Publishers, 2004), pp45-48.

the great variety of scenarios in which mentoring may be happening. It is easier to describe what mentoring is not, although it is important to understand what is entailed in a fruitful and beneficial mentoring relationship. Lewis refers to unintentional relationships, which are often mistakenly called 'mentoring', where certain individuals may be called 'mentors' just because they serve as role models or inspire others to Christian maturity. He says this is misleading;[96] while mentoring may occur in non-formal structures, it is the case that an effective mentoring relationship is one arrived at through a deliberate, conscious, informed and purposed arrangement, a view shared by both mentoring writers Mallison and Pue.[97] The mentoring relationship is not a gossip-driven forum, neither is it a means to providing release from stress. When a mentee presents their challenges before a mentor, it is not the expectation that they will be harangued for any failings, but that they will be helped to develop the skills necessary to overcome these challenges.

Mentoring should help lead to the spiritual growth of the individual and to the wider objective of the growth of God's kingdom. In a foreword to *Mentoring Matters*, Martin Robinson points out two reasons for mentoring. Firstly, the physical mobility of populations has reduced the availability of natural, local mentors. Secondly, related to mobility, is the shift in ideas and related ideologies.[98] This

---

[96] Lewis, *Mentoring Matters*, p21.

[97] Mallison, *Mentoring: To Develop Disciples & Leaders*, pp169-170; Pue, *Mentoring Leaders Wisdom for Developing, Calling, and Competency*, p193.

[98] Lewis, *Mentoring Matters*, p5.

reflects the situation in African diaspora churches in the Yorkshire area, and other immigrant situations. Members of these African churches are mainly migrants who have come to the United Kingdom and chosen to settle permanently or temporarily in Yorkshire. In some cases, some of these members may have been born in the United Kingdom and form a new generation of African expatriates or professionals. For most of them, leaving their family and church environments has meant loss of access to their natural mentors, and therefore there is a need for new sources of learning in order to grow and flourish. In this it is necessary to recognise that natural mentors or informal mentorships are not invalid, but that they are essentially weak.[99] According to the mentoring writer Viv Thomas, people need new knowledge and the reshaping of their ideas if they are to continue to grow. [100] In addition, mobility has meant that they have come into a different geographical, ideological, political and cultural setting leading to a shift in ideas and culture.

The need for mentoring is obvious in this situation. The alternative to mentoring is training that might be more expensive and less flexible, and which lacks the personal interaction enjoyed within mentoring practice. An immediate value in mentoring lies in its capacity to equip new and emergent or potential leaders with the necessary skills and knowledge to face and deal with the challenges posed by their new environment. Part of the purpose of mentoring is to enable both the mentor and the mentee to

---

[99] Lewis, *Mentoring Matters*, p21.

[100] Viv Thomas, *Future Leaders* (Carlisle: Paternoster Press, 1999), p146.

rise to the various challenges that the mentee may face as they develop a multicultural community. 'Mentors are often used by God as one of the most significant means of assisting leaders during times of challenge.' [101] Cultural shock brought about by relocation to a new country can prove to be a challenge. The multicultural context can ferment a multiplicity of cultural 'shocks', and recourse to good-quality, experienced mentoring can help mitigate this. The support of a mentor is likely to help develop someone into a new leader with the skill set necessary for them to maintain or plant a new church even in unfamiliar territory.

Because mentoring might seem to be a friendly relationship, it is tempting to gloss over the serious and critical nature of skills and values being brought to the fore. Christian mentoring should neither be accidental nor haphazard. It is meant to be purpose driven, and it is not meant as a policing strategy. As Lewis observes, it is both a personal and spiritual investment. [102] Any mentoring arrangement requires the commitment of time, expertise and planning, and even other resources.

Mentoring will assist potential leaders to have an intimate relationship with God who has called them to ministry, to have fellowship and not feel isolated in ministry, and to have somebody to confer with outside their own situation. One value of mentoring is that it helps new leaders to avoid the pitfalls or mistakes other leaders before them may have made. Further, in itself, the mentoring process will also help them to acquire specific

[101] Pue, *Mentoring Leaders*, p224.

[102] Lewis, *Mentoring Matters*, p22.

knowledge and experience of mentoring which will then enable them to mentor others in their local churches. This will result in multiplication as the skills of mentoring are spread widely. Krallmann recognises this when he says, 'Leadership development in Christ's name ought to be undertaken with keen awareness of this dimension of multiplication so recognizable in Christ's ministry.'[103]

However, to appreciate this in the specific context of African churches in Europe, there are some concerns that, if addressed, could lead to more growth. The leaders' educational background, their understanding of mission strategy for church growth and their training is often not satisfactory. Even though a number of African church leaders are motivated to reach out, the majority do not see the value of establishing links with indigenous community churches which would result in better cross-cultural relationships and church growth, the reasons for which will now be explored.

Reflection

- *What are the advantages of the mentoring process for:*

    a) Spiritual growth?

    b) Professional growth as a culturally intelligent leader?

---

[103] Krallmann, *Mentoring for Mission*, p188.

Chapter Nine

Cross-cultural Need for Mentoring and How to Journey with Others

Addressing the question of cross-cultural relationships is a matter of need for most African diaspora churches, especially as they begin to lay the foundation for developing new leaders. The church growth writers Stevens and Collins describe how each church contains a genetic code which determines at the time it is founded what the church will become. They write:

> A church that starts with certain assumptions about the nature of the fellowship, style of leadership, the place of ordained and theologically trained leadership, and the mission of the church in society will find it very difficult, though not impossible, to change the genetic code later.[104]

The value of mentoring in part is to seek to influence this genetic code. Ethiopian and Eritrean churches in Yorkshire, as is the case with most African-led Pentecostal churches, identify themselves as having a mission to

---

[104] R Paul Stevens and Phil Collins, *The Equipping Pastor* (West Bethesda, MD: Alban Institute, 1993), p51.

preach the good news to the host nation. These churches need to realise that engaging effectively with British culture requires a new mindset to mitigate against any possible adverse foundational assumptions. For example, some discussion in missional literature highlights the need for Christianity to reclaim secular space. In an African mindset, this may be taken to imply that it should be desecularised, whereas in the literature it means to invest it with more of a spiritual consciousness that takes into account the importance of God to His world.

Developing new leaders helps to bridge the chasm between the initial founding assumptions and the missional demands of the new context. When both indigenous and missional churches engage in cross-cultural initiatives to promote better and greater church growth, they should then progress from the Homogeneous Unit Principle to the Heterogeneous Principle of church growth, from a mono-ethnic community to a multi-ethnic community for whom mission is the heartbeat. The Homogenous Unit Principle is the basis on which most expatriate churches begin, namely that of reaching out to and incorporating people from a similar cultural and ethnic background, whereas the Heterogeneous Principle seeks to incorporate people across backgrounds as New Testament teaching demands (see Galatians 3:26-29). Mentoring provides the maturity and depth critical to unleashing growth capable of making this transition.

Examples of where cross-cultural mentoring can help

Leadership styles and attitudes to children's ministry are just two areas where cross-cultural input can make a significant difference to African immigrant churches' ability to both reach the host culture and disciple their next generation.

Currently, in some Ethiopian and Eritrean churches, church leaders seem to be doing things in their own way, with the pastor acting as the final arbiter of what is right and wrong. This trend can be seen in other African Pentecostal churches where the pastor is the founder and chief executive. This derives from what is often termed the 'man of God' culture that comes from high-power distance cultures. It is an artefact of migrant cultures of this type, and it can take time for this view to change. Obviously this would be a real challenge in a multicultural church, and it certainly would be hard for Westerners to understand or accept. Changing such a 'man of God' model would be hard and would need to be addressed in an empathetic manner by a monocultural church's culturally intelligent leader. A conversation about a change in expectations of leadership would be needed, but it would take much more than a simple expectation that it would address the issue. In reality, some kind of change process would need to be implemented where the church's leadership team would slowly model an increasingly egalitarian leadership style with an attendant sense of a kind of democracy, where members take responsibility for decision-making with the leader/s.

In churches led by the 'man of God', most are supported by a committee of trustees or elders who are 'yes men'. In this kind of situation, Willard warns, '[Leaders] who say, "It's just between me and God," or "What I do is my own business," have misunderstood God as well as themselves.'[105] 'The man of God' culture will need to be challenged effectively if these kinds of congregations are to be transformed. If a leader is to effectively transform the communities they are seeking to reach for Christ, they must also experience transformation. An effective mentoring relationship is therefore a transformational relationship.

Another factor to bear in mind in most of these churches in the United Kingdom is that the family size is expanding, but in some of these churches there is no noticeable children's ministry and no strategy to develop this for the future. This is often because of a lesser appreciation by immigrant churches of the need to invest in children's ministry, particularly in a Western culture which will not pass on a Christendom DNA outside the church. Some African nations are very much like a former Christendom Europe, where children pick up a degree of Christian culture from broader interaction with society, and immigrant churches can assume that things are the same in the UK.

Another issue faced by migrant first-generation churches is that they can bring a cultural assumption that children need to become like their more mature adult counterparts, rather than be focused on separately. In this

---

[105] Dallas Willard, *Renovation of the Heart: Putting on the Character of Christ* (Leicester: IVP, 2002), pp150-151.

sense, the goal is to become a kind of mini-adult, rather like the caricature of Victorian culture where children were to be seen but not heard. However, in the West, the view of children has largely been reversed and there are no wider societal pressures on children to blend in with adult culture. As a result, these first-generation immigrant churches must be open to changing their approach, otherwise their children will not be discipled effectively in monocultural congregations of this type.

There is a pressing need to recognise that so-called third-culture children are a priority if we are to reach the next generation and, in the process, raise up a new generation of leaders. Children of reverse missionaries are in danger of growing up divorced from both their home culture and the host culture in favour of an identity-light third culture, yet they could become one of our most significant bridgeheads into the adoptive culture that we are trying to reach if this divorce could be kept from happening. The earlier third-culture children can be effectively discipled and shaped to be proud of the strengths that their blend of cultures bring, the more secure they will be in identity and therefore faith. The churches that do this well will hopefully enable children and young people to better identify with their churches and families; they will encourage them to see their faith communities as a resource to help them adapt to life in the West and influence its emerging culture with the gospel, rather than hindering them.

Mentoring – a unique catalyst to mission

Mentoring can help leaders to see opening doors and spot the new people possibilities. [106] The gaps that exist in African churches at present are timely opportunities for mission, with mentoring the catalyst that opens these doors of opportunity. As a catalytic process, mentoring preserves the respect and dignity of mentees; at the same time, experience-sharing helps bring about maturity. A mentee grows in wisdom gained from a mentor's experiences. This may help develop skills to be used in identifying possibilities for church planting.

Leaders need friendship and encouragement as well as training in ministry skills. Specifically, most African leaders in the United Kingdom would benefit from higher education, but the current instability around education in general may result in a leadership skills shortage. Gibbs and Coffey also make this point in their remarks about the general state of theological education in the Western world.[107] Whatever the outcome, the value of mentoring in the development of new leaders is such that it can be embedded as standard practice in missional contexts and training. The basic value of mentoring to a new leader is that they have someone to stand by them as a critical friend. The mentor facilitates or enables skills to be developed or sharpened. 'It's lonely at the top' is an often-quoted phrase that is also true in Christian ministry.

---

[106] Viv Thomas, *Future Leaders* (Carlisle: Paternoster Press, 1999), p147.

[107] Eddie Gibbs and Ian Coffey, *Church Next: Quantum Changes in Christian Ministry* (Westmont, IL: IVP, 2001), p93.

Reflection

- *How do you respond to the idea of a mentor as 'a critical friend'?*

- *Outline a scenario in your own ministry where such a relationship would be helpful.*

- *Identify a relationship where you might be the 'critical friend' in order to develop someone else's ministry.*

Mentoring and goal orientation

Mentoring helps leaders to develop their relationship with God and engage with His will. Mallison shows the importance of mentoring in developing spiritual growth as it helps a person to recognise and respond to the Holy Spirit.[108] Mentors assist leaders to develop habits that help them to achieve their goals. As Clinton and Clinton have stated, the mentee responds to 'your mentor knowing that he/she is moving you toward that goal'.[109] This is the ultimate task placed upon the mentor: helping the mentee achieve their goal. In the missional context, it consists of leading them to 'make disciples of all nations' (Matthew 28:19). Making disciples becomes a habit, a normal and routine feature of church planting. The mentee is only effective in mission if their leadership potential is fully developed with help from a skilled mentor working under the gifting of the Holy Spirit. The mentoring relationship is

---

[108] Mallison, *Mentoring: To Develop Disciples & Leaders*, p47.
[109] J Robert Clinton and Richard W Clinton, *The Mentor Handbook* (Altadena, CA: Barnabas Publishers, 1991), p23.

a reciprocal up-building relationship (1 Thessalonians 5:11). Both mentor and mentee enter into a voluntary and deliberate agreement in obedience to the Holy Spirit and for Christ to build His Church. However, developing new leaders suggests looking at and attempting to address problems that will happen in the future.

New leaders are not tasked to resolve past issues; rather, today's leaders need to be orientated towards tomorrow's expected growth. It is not possible to solve problems based on a simple understanding of what caused them; more understanding is required. In other words, the cause of a problem is not likely to be its solution; in fact, it is likely to multiply the problem. However, to deal with a problem's root and symptoms, the solution needs to be different from the cause; it can only come from fresh thinking. Christian mentoring recognises that to err is human, but it also accepts that God's grace and creativity are needed for problem solving. Indeed, Christian mentoring is about extending the kingdom of God, as the mentoring thinkers Clinton and Clinton put it:

> Mentoring guides and challenges the mentoree toward leadership values which accumulate into ministry philosophy that will lead to effective ministry and a unique contribution to the kingdom of God over the life time.[110]

---

[110] Clinton and Clinton, *The Mentor Handbook*, pp4-14.

Guide to setting goals

Remember:

- Ministry goals are about what the mentee hopes to achieve in their ministry field training in a given year.

- Coaching goals are about what the mentee hopes to learn through the coaching process in a given year.

- Mentoring goals are about what a mentee hopes to become through the whole life experience of a given year.

Process

Before the mentee's first meeting, they need to think through and suggest goals – what they hope to achieve, learn or become. This encourages ownership and commitment to the goals. One sentence per goal is enough. The mentor needs to review student suggestions and, in discussion, hone them into effective statements of desired outcomes that may be achieved in ministry practice. The goal-setting process may take the whole of a first session with an individual.

Good goals are:

S – specific (naming areas and issues to address)

M – measurable (so that progress can be discerned)

A – achievable (within the year-long process)

C – consistent (with development as missional)

SMAC goals also need to be time bound – in other words, by what point might they be achieved? Hence, setting goals has future mentoring meetings in mind, and a monitoring process can be readily established by SMAC goals.

Mentoring that creates mutuality

According to Mallison, mentoring is an important way of helping the leader to develop disciples and other leaders. His view is strongly linked to an appreciation of the importance of a leader being a good relational mentor. Consider his comments below when discussing how to develop good mentoring relationships:

> Seek to be transparent with each other. Don't force this, just let the Spirit lead you gently! Share your disappointments and frustration and celebrate together your joys and successes.
>
> In seeking to deepen your degree of vulnerability and intimacy with each other, understanding the five levels of communication on which people relate can be helpful. These move from the least to the most intimate.
>
> 'Level 1 – Stereotyped or hackneyed expressions:' In this stage of communication, little of meaning is communicated about a person's real thoughts or feelings.
>
> 'Level 2 – Communication of facts:' Factual communication does not focus on things that are felt deeply, or are deeply meaningful to a person.

Rather, simple statements are made that distance the communicator from saying anything that exposes their real self. Little risk is taken in what is disclosed, meaning the communicator does not make themselves vulnerable to criticism.

'Level 3 – Disclosing ideas and judgments:' The disclosure of a person's real thoughts or ideas is based on a willingness to trust that the listener will not reject everything that is communicated, or the person themselves.

'Level 4 – Revealing feelings:' The revelation of personal feelings is a risky business that requires deeper trust. This level is only reached when such trust exists.

'Level 5 – Oneness:' This stage is idealistic to some extent, but when a friendship or relationship reaches a high degree on interpersonal reciprocated trust, then there is a sense of unity between the people concerned. In this case there is a feeling that people at this stage are on each other's side – looking out for their best interests even if at times they have to offer feedback that may challenge a friend for good.

As Christians, we believe this unique experience of communion with each other is produced by being fully open to the presence of the Holy Spirit in our friendships.[111]

---

[111] Mallison, *Mentoring: To Develop Disciples & Leaders*, p56.

Mallison also highlights major areas that mentoring, or indeed coaching, might help facilitate:

- Developing the spiritual life
- Helping the right focus to maximise quality time with those closest to a person
- Setting priorities and goals
- Choosing the good and the best in the person's life
- Personal and professional development
- Attitude towards and use of money
- Handling power with humility and grace
- Sexual relationships
- Remaining open and honest
- Coping with stress
- Keeping positive and hopeful
- Self-control
- Resolving conflicts

Leadership formation

The person who helps other people to achieve their potential may already be a leader. In developing new leaders, the Church is made up of all sorts of people from varied backgrounds. African churches do not advertise leadership vacancies; they choose instead to engage personnel from within. Sometimes, especially in small or emergent churches, the available pool of leadership candidates may be so thin that leaders have to be chosen and developed from those deemed to be less gifted. In this case, a mentor with the ability to maximise these young leaders' potential for mission will be essential.

The need for great mentors is as real as is the need for cross-cultural mission. What has been said largely suggests that the benefits of mentoring are skewed in favour of the mentee but, as in most relationships, the benefits are mutual. The mentor also benefits because the role in which they are placed is one of trust and favour. In mission, therefore, the mentor is called to a position of privilege, helping to empower co-workers through developing or fermenting leadership skills. Further, the mentor is always learning new things from their mentees.

A mentee will from time to time bring a new or fresh perspective to the mentoring relationship. Such moments can bring very strong learning on the part of the mentor. New perspectives will serve to fruitfully engage the mentor, helping to add to an already rich body of experience. This is affirmed by Wright's observation that mentors 'who are blind to their own weaknesses, prejudices or insecurities can be a risk'.[112] Further, current mentoring practices in some African churches are arbitrary since the pastor or mentor is the final arbiter of right and wrong. This in part stems from the definitions of mentoring discussed earlier, which places the mentor in a high position. Yet the truth is that mentoring also provides the mentor with an opportunity for accountability. This is important in those cases where the church structure is such

[112] Walter C Wright Jr, *Mentoring: The Promise of Relational Leadership* (Milton Keynes: Paternoster Press, 2004), p33.

that the pastor is the most senior person, making decisions without the benefit of trustees or elders.[113] On the other hand, pastors, who are often deemed to be the church leaders, can find themselves in effective mission by using their invaluable experience to establish new leaders through an empowering mentoring relationship.

Only secure leaders give power to others while also encouraging them to fulfil their own kinds of ministry. A confident pastor will not hesitate to train or mentor another person to be a pastor. In order to develop effective new leadership, then, leaders should develop other leaders by giving the people for whom they are responsible the space to fail and learn. Mentors are often used to develop a leader's abilities. Effective mentors beget effective leaders. The mentor is a leader engaged in the task of developing leaders. In undertaking this task, the mentor and mentee recognise that mentoring is not mistake-proof, but is a maturing journey.

In the mentoring relationship, the mentor may be as vulnerable as the mentee. The thinker Wright gives a useful account of his experience with his mentor George Ladd.[114] Ladd possesses brilliance but shows vulnerability and the pain of life, a lonely man who teaches about community but struggles to sustain his own relationships. Here we see the mentor in both his strengths and his weaknesses, and realise that he is not perfect, just human. It is therefore wise to understand that even the experienced and mature leader, as Lewis puts it, has moments of

---

[113] Walter Wright, *Relational Leadership*, p202.
[114] Wright, *Mentoring: The Promise of Relational Leadership*, pp31-32.

hesitation, just like a young leader.[115] Their experience is exposed, as is the mentee's inexperience. By bringing that experience into the relationship, the mentor also begins to make themselves accountable to the mentee. Once the mentoring relationship is appreciated in this light, it begins to cultivate or nurture the humanity of the relationship, bringing value and maturity to a developmental process. In this way, mentoring becomes a reciprocal, mutual relationship. It acknowledges that all leaders are subject to a higher authority, that of Jesus, and the mentoring relationship is itself managed by the most senior of advocates, promised by Jesus: the Holy Spirit (John 16:7ff). This view of mentoring fits in with the model of mentoring referred to as a Triadic relationship.[116] The point is that Christian mentoring is a gift of Christ to enable mission to grow and to reach every part of the world.

Reflection

Leadership development is a two-way process.

- *Suggest ways in which the mentoring relationship enhances leadership development for both mentor and mentee.*

- *Can you see yourself benefiting from such a relationship?*

---

[115] Lewis, *Mentoring Matters*, p23.

[116] Lewis, *Mentoring Matters*, p20.

Structure – putting an agreed process in place

We need to put an agreed process in place in order to facilitate an effective mentoring relationship that will enable us to put talent and ministry gifts together to multiply mission in a multicultural context in the UK, starting from the base of African diaspora churches. To begin with, each leader who intends to buy into the mentoring process will need vision, passion and commitment.

Vision is the starting point, but without a clear plan for implementation it will only be a dream. Therefore, that leader should move from a plan to form a mission partnership with others who are also committed to the process. My observation so far is that there are many African reverse missionaries armed with a vision, but few have indicated who is walking with them to realise that vision. They are surrounded by many helpers, but these helpers do not give the guidance and space for loyal, trusted and dependable reflection which comes from mentoring.

In order to achieve the vision they have, they need mentoring as part of mission partnership. It would help immensely if this partnership were forged in a cross-cultural context in which African church leaders work together with indigenous church leaders who have mission experience and who have sought to engage imaginatively with their native context. There is much room for misunderstanding and miscommunication at this point, but it is well worth persisting, since such relationships carry great promise for the future of multicultural church growth that mirrors the values and theological commitment of our New Testament predecessors. Such mission-centred partnerships are the best vehicle for equipping both our own churches and those of our indigenous brethren for biblical mission. It is in this context that we will be able to develop frameworks for mentoring the rising generation of church leaders and missionaries.

The next step should be to arrive at a series of questions distilled from experience that could lead to the formulation of guidelines that might help potential mentors in their task. But how do we identify these rising mentors in the first place? In part, they will be self-selected in that the mentee needs to find someone they can trust, but who will also be willing to challenge their perceptions. Indeed, this needs to be a two-way process, since the mentee may well challenge the mentor's approach, too. The important thing is that both will be engaged in a process of discovery.

Here we need to touch on a potentially sensitive issue: too often, African church leaders and missionaries defer to the opinions and perspectives of the leader(s) of the church from which they originally came in their home country. This is all well and good – it is right to honour and respect those who brought us to faith. However, those distant leaders do not know and possibly cannot read the situation in contemporary Europe, and are likely to believe that what works at home is bound to work in the new context. This cannot be allowed to formulate the mentee's approach to mission in their new context, and allowance needs to be made for their new circumstances. It is all too easy to see mission in Europe through culturally tinted lenses that may in fact distort the process.

The mentee will need to put their activity through the same grid, beginning with a clear vision of what is wanted and needed from their mentor. This vision, in turn, needs to be forged in a mission-centred partnership both with the mentor and the church or congregation to which they are answerable, and so it can become the basis for equipping the emerging church or congregation to produce mentors and mentees, thus extending the process in a biblical fashion.

Timelines

The process above mirrors what Paul did with Timothy when he said, 'And the things you have heard me say in the presence of many witnesses entrust to reliable people who will also be qualified to teach others' (2 Timothy 2:2, NIV UK). You will notice that in this example the mentoring process extends to a third generation, but there is no reason to suppose that Paul intended the chain to end there; rather, it was meant to continue until Christ returns to fully and finally establish His kingdom in power. Paul is not talking about random people passing on the message, but a considered process. Timothy is assumed to have listened – not just casually heard, but really paid attention in order to seek out reliable people. The definition of 'reliable' here is that they should be qualified to teach. This implies a considered and deliberate process of training or teaching, and we know that the teaching method of both Jesus and Paul was, in the rabbinic tradition, to mentor disciples to take over mission functions.

From the outset, it is necessary for both mentor and mentee to set out the terms of the relationship and to establish an agreed timeline for the partnership. A younger leader may benefit from a mentor with the appropriate experience to give at least a year's commitment to the relationship, with an agreement to continue for longer upon an annual review of progress and suitability of the relationship. In this way, it is possible to build accountability into the relationship and to set out expectations on both sides. We have found the mentoring relationship works best when it is based on an action/reflection learning model such that the mentee takes agreed actions and later regroups with their mentor to reflect upon and learn from the process.

Action

- *Identify possible mentoring relationships that might benefit:*
  - a) *Your own ministry*
  - b) *The ministry of junior colleagues*
  - c) *The mission of your church*
- *Think about a timeline for bringing this about.*

My journey in *missio Dei* in the United Kingdom

The process above can be understood from the following brief account of my own journey of partnership in service for the kingdom of God in the UK. I arrived in the UK on

5th December, 2002. The following year, in 2003, I worked within the Ethiopian community, often going to public places such as bus and train stations to befriend Ethiopian and Eritrean people and engage with them for the gospel. Clearly this was not reaching the host culture.

Later I met with Andrew Hinds, who became important to help me take the initial steps in my role as a reverse missionary and church planter. Andrew was an associate pastor at the Leeds South Parade Baptist Church, although he serves today as a West Yorkshire police officer. Such an initial contact is necessary as it may offer a framework for sensitivity to the Holy Spirit's urgings that comes from a person or persons through whom God can offer insights or help. Andrew was a good friend rather than a mentor. This was a phase in which the Amharic-speaking church was being established and networking was being developed, but there was no pronounced initiative towards multi-ethnic missional community development. However, my relationship with Andrew, and with others like him, proved to be important in helping me to consider the benefits of intercultural interaction and develop my thinking.

In 2007, a powerful divine connection was forged with Dr Martin Robinson. He was the bridge to the next level of partnership formation, opening a door into the Fellowship of the Churches of Christ. The connection was not expected, but it was the kind of relationship that I had hoped to form. It proved to be a critical step in the development of my vision, which was not just about church planting but also about training and equipping leaders for mission. From the first day I began courses with

Martin, I experienced some of the most important learning which has contributed to my journey in missional leadership. He made a connection with me particularly because he answered the kinds of questions I was really asking. A reverse missionary can feel so alone, but my link with Martin made me feel connected. Questions were addressed and I felt I had begun to discover the way forward in my work in the UK. Martin did not offer monetary support, but knowledge as well as empathy to the questions of my heart and mind.

David Judson, a former Middle East missionary, was also important to my journey on the MA, as he helped me to develop my English writing skills. It was very important for me to develop these as they have helped me to better express myself in the British host culture I now belong to.

It is also important to mention how Martin was a bridge to many other partnerships, especially the one with Dr Richard Whitehouse, with whom I developed the *Multiply*[117] course. Dr Whitehouse offered at this level a friendship and informal mentoring which helped me settle in the Fellowship of the Churches of Christ. The *Multiply* course would help emerging leaders in the churches I was participating in planting, so it addressed issues to help equip them to work more effectively in the context of Western British culture. I also learned from his personal mission approach, centring on the equipping of others, which was necessary to help me understand the multicultural context of the UK as well as to further develop my vision.

---

[117] ForMission, Multiply, Birmingham: ForMission College.

In 2011, I embarked on a new and demanding challenge as part of my calling. This was to start a learning centre in Leeds, despite my limitations, such as capacity, experience in higher education management, and even the multicultural environment in which I was finding myself. It was then that my prayers for a colleague were answered when in March 2012 I struck up friendship with Dr Clement Katulushi from Zambia. What endeared me to him was his humility and willingness to work with me in realising my vision. It was through this connection that I was able to accomplish some of my goals, including the establishment of our ForMission campus in Leeds. His ability to understand education was an important help to the development of students as future reverse missionary leaders.

Fulfilling a vision requires God's provision. Only God can bring the right people to help pursue that vision.

Reflecting on these relationships, I have had the space to consult and think through various situations with both Dr Whitehouse and Dr Katulushi informally as mentors. Although Dr Robinson also played the important role of a father figure, on one hand Richard Whitehouse has acted as an informal mentor and a good friend, and on the other hand Clement Katulushi has continued to help me pursue the vision.

What all of this demonstrates is that each of us invests deeply in one another in our Lord Jesus Christ across ethnic and cultural divides. We all grow as we share our gifts and experience. And all of those I mention have also deeply appreciated the fellowship we have all shared on our journeys.

Hence, I would say that these have been necessary partnerships which in themselves prepared me for the current phase where I have a professional mentor, Dr Rick Lewis. I entered a formal mentoring relationship with Dr Lewis in 2015, a journey which continues today. This relationship is critical to facilitating the vision I had while God spoke to me in Ethiopia, and the journey I started on 5th December 2002 in the United Kingdom.

As the saying goes, if you want to go fast, go on your own; if you want to go far, go with others; if you lead too fast, nobody follows. The lesson to leaders is that there is a need for mentors, and the journey to developing multi-ethnic communities for mission is not meant to be a solo journey.

Reflection

- *Having read about my experience, now draw your own timeline and reflect on how you might improve on your ministry journey.*

- *In what ways is accountability important for personal, spiritual and professional development?*

Action

- *Consider sharing what you have learned so far with other leaders.*

- *Make plans to implement a mentoring process:*

    a) *For yourself*

    b) *For your church leaders and potential leaders*

    c) *For your network*

Conclusion

In the first part of this book, my argument has been that the leader is one who sees clearly where the church needs to go and has the vision and ability to take it there. The leader is not primarily involved in 'maintenance' but in 'mission'. They are an entrepreneur rather than a caretaker. They are a people-person who inspires their followers to become missional by example and by teaching. As the leadership writer Walter Wright points out, 'The leader invests in the growth and development of the followers, empowering them to become what God has gifted them to be.'[118] To achieve this, the leader will need both character and skills. Character without skills may produce direction without movement; skills without character will result in failure because there will be lack of persistence or the ability to integrate the skills to bring results.

In short, the missional leader needs to show commitment and sacrifice. It is helpful to understand the importance of passion in the leader and in the process of forming multi-ethnic communities for mission. Paul's initial calling was to the Gentiles, but his passion for his own people was so overpowering that he was willing to be cursed and even cut off from Christ for the salvation of his own people (Romans 9:3). His commitment was so

---

[118] Wright, *Relational Leadership*, p44.

absolute that he sought no personal gain or advantage in his endeavours and was prepared to sacrifice his freedom and personal comforts to preach the gospel.

Additionally essential are gifts that come from the Holy Spirit. These include vision, passion and commitment. Skills that mark a culturally intelligent leader may be natural or acquired, and will include such things as cultural literacy, relational intelligence, emotional intelligence, creative intelligence, team formation, conflict management experience and so on. Both qualities and skills are important for the leader in a multi-ethnic community. However, when skills become dominant or overemphasised, little or no fruit will be produced; the gift of the Holy Spirit will be suffocated or stifled. When qualities are used at a high degree or level or released fully, then skills will become manifested.

The need to recognise both qualities and skills in the multicultural community is a prerequisite for dealing with conflict. Pastors or church leaders who claim the prerogative of the gift of the Holy Spirit at the expense or neglect of necessary skills usually lack training and can be bigots and even abusive in their leadership. Similarly, leaders who claim the superiority of skills and qualifications and ignore the gift of the Holy Spirit are likely to bring about a 'deadening' of the community and extinguish its vitality and life force and that which makes it missional and multi-ethnic. There is need, therefore, to maintain a healthy balance between qualities and skills in the leader.

In the second part of the book, 'Moving from Monocultural Maintenance to Multi-ethnic Missional

Communities: The *Kairos* time!', we concluded our survey that the gospel is God's salvation plan for the whole world, so it cannot differentiate between cultures. It regards all cultures, and all the people within them, as equally tainted by sin and equally in need of redemption. The gospel is above culture. Jesus was born as a Jew into a specific culture which God had prepared to reach out to all nations. He was to be a light to the Gentiles as well as the glory of His people Israel. Therefore, the thrust of this book is that the time for mono-ethnic church planting is past. Now is the appointed time for leaders to shift from mono-church communities and embark unreservedly on planting and developing multi-ethnic communities for mission. And thereafter, we have seen the importance of multi-ethnic church planting as so many people are not active church members and are ignorant of the gospel.

To plant churches successfully, the church, first of all, needs to have a vision and passion for church planting. A key element in building multi-ethnic missional communities, implied in the first part of this book, is to do with vision. The church planter must allow his vision to bear images of what will be. Church planting requires leaders to 'see'. Seeing what God is doing requires sanctified imagination. Here are three examples of what is meant by 'imagination':

- In the Old Testament, God takes Abraham outside, shows him the night sky and tells him that his descendants will be as many as the stars (Genesis 15:5).

- The physicist Isaac Newton sat outside in a garden under a tree and, when an apple fell on him, the theory of gravity was conceived.

- In Luke 10 we see Jesus' power of imagination as He appointed the seventy-two, already visualising multiplication growth. He imagined, indeed saw, the devil struck down like a bolt of lightning, because of the work of the team that He had established, under the anointing of the Holy Spirit.

The word 'imagination' is as abstract as it is physical. It is the power not only to see but also to conceive that which has yet to be seen. Imagination is to visualise, to have a vision of that which could or will or ought to be, to have an 'image'. The monocultural community does not excite the same sense of colour and enrichment as does the multicultural community. Imagination sees in the multicultural community the breadth and scope of how the mission of God embraces His desire for a deeper fellowship with all nations.

However, church planting must be targeted and purposed especially into establishing multi-ethnic communities for mission. Recognition of the merits of the multicultural community so far is something worth celebrating. Just the very act of coming together and meeting to seek the Lord's face as people from different cultural backgrounds is a merit.

The multi-ethnic community offers to missional agents a new sense of flexibility that is inherent in the manner of achieving set goals. This flexibility enables the imagination, creativity and gifting of each member to be appreciated and to grow. The multi-ethnic community should not operate a rigid structure, but instead ought to encourage an approach that is relational or relationship-based. This can lead to a heightened sensitivity to the Holy Spirit and to how the members are responding to the challenges faced in individual situations.

Church planting without the energy of the Holy Spirit is dead. There is a need for refuelling. Whereas a missional community might possess tremendous assets and be rich in the calibre of its people, the most likely cultural danger for Western churches is the over-systematisation of imagination, creativity and the lack of an environment which allows the Holy Spirit to be active.

Another attendant problem is that our way of learning has tended to make us doubt that which our 'mere eyes' see, to the detriment of our 'inner eyes', our imagination. This has made us feel that we are too well educated for the Holy Spirit to dwell in us and lead us along the way we should go. We need to be able to empty ourselves to allow an infilling of the Holy Spirit. And it is for this reason that some of us are where we are now; we are like racing drivers making a pit stop to fill up, change tyres and get ready to go again.

The possibility here is that the entire process of planting churches is put under the charge of the Holy Spirit. Imagination is vital, but the Holy Spirit should also be at work in us. What we imagine, the image before us, the vision deposited in us, should be none other than by the Spirit. The work of the early Christians could not proceed without the presence of the Holy Spirit! Jesus gave His followers the promise of the Holy Spirit, and once He made good His promise, growth became a reality. Likewise, the only success church planters can see is that which comes through the Holy Spirit.

As we have seen, church planters need to make the right preparations. This will involve identifying the right area for planting the church, gifted leaders to do the job and willing members to join them. Researching the area, planning carefully and training the team will all help the work to succeed, and to lead on to the planting of yet more churches. But above all, prayer will be needed, since church planting is the Lord's work rather than humanity's. As Jesus said, 'I will build my church, and the gates of Hades will not overcome it' (Matthew 16:18, NIV UK).

The place of reverse mission and mentoring formed the third part of this book. The lessons drawn from current practices in reverse mission are stark. It is the expectation that those engaged in reverse mission are called to reach the majority, or host community, for Christ. However, in reality, the situation is different; most churches started by reverse missionaries largely serve members drawn from their own ethnic communities. This cannot be true reverse mission. It is not enough to reach one's fellow countrymen and not engage with the host community. Developing multi-ethnic communities for mission is therefore the direction reverse missionaries ought to take.

There is clearly a necessity for mentoring, for journeying with others, and there are lessons to be drawn from experiences of developing multicultural communities within the African diaspora churches. The value of mentoring as a means of developing new leaders for those churches cannot be denied.

Like other Africans, Ethiopians and Eritreans are widely dispersed in many countries around the world. However, there is little or no deliberate organised or agreed and planned mentoring structure in place for existing or emergent leaders. In some other African churches, as the specific mission context, some form of mentoring has been practised, but this mentoring is not adequate for addressing the needs, aspirations and challenges of cross-cultural growth. Mentoring is a critical ingredient in developing new leaders, but its value is such that mentoring is necessary even for the present leadership to begin to attend to present-day problems and shortfalls. Commonly, in the countries where I have travelled for ministry, I have noticed that the mentoring deficiency noted above is identical to the situation in Britain.

For any further development to happen, planning is essential. As Sanders remarks, 'The intentionality of starting early with developing future leaders resulted in success of biblical proportion.'[119] Such success is neither instant nor accidental. It is timely and planned. Developing missional leaders should start at the very beginning of mission, as growing leadership should be a daily aspirational process. The expected growth will be representative of how this leadership has been sown. Epic growth is sown early. However, the usefulness of mentoring is such that yesterday's omissions and failures can become invaluable lessons when mentoring new leaders for the present and future generations.

---

[119] Sanders, *The Power of Mentoring*, p143.

The present leadership should realise that they have an obligation for the future. 'One of the key roles of top-level leadership is to intentionally develop the next generation of leaders in order to keep the operation running successfully.'[120] Mentoring a possible successor (or successors) should be done by every leader for the purpose of continuing their ministry and promoting its growth.[121]

There are a number of benefits to be gained in establishing mentoring in order to develop new leaders. Among these is the fact that mentoring itself produces leaders who in turn develop more leaders. The knock-on effect of producing leaders is that the challenges of mission become less difficult; instead, growth becomes real. This is encapsulated in the observation 'to add growth, lead followers – to multiply, lead leaders'.[122]

Finally, it might seem impractical to develop multi-ethnic missional communities given that, to date, few people have advanced arguments in favour of such communities. Further, some thinkers have argued that the merits of establishing multi-ethnic missional communities are debatable and are inclined to discourage a move towards them. However, the formation of multi-ethnic missional communities is inevitable. I see the Church in Great Britain and elsewhere in the Western world being transformed, not just the establishment of churches with

---

[120] Sanders, *The Power of Mentoring*, p141.

[121] Sanders, *The Power of Mentoring*, p144.

[122] John C Maxwell, *The 21 Irrefutable Laws of Leadership: Follow Them and People Will Follow You* (Nashville, TN: Thomas Nelson Publishers, 1998), p205.

minority ethnic groups. Such a Church will be truly missional, in the sense of 'sent' by God.

I can see that the Church will become multi-ethnic. It will be a community, not just of one nation, but one embracing many nations; not just one ethnic group, but all peoples. At such a time, books like this will become redundant, consigned to history.

The Church will only be a community when we are all feeding from one communion, the Lord's table. The onus is on scholars, theologians, practitioners and all those whom Christ has called to be His witnesses, to think not only about the monocultural community, but more vigorously about how to develop and engage with the soon-coming multi-ethnic community.

The recommendations made in this book for you to act upon

- Gather a multi-ethnic leadership.

- Develop catalytic qualities and primary skills for multicultural leadership.

- Move from mono to multicultural missional communities.

- Begin church planting in a new-culture context – this means adopting a new approach to church planting, engaging host culture and immigrant churches in a common task through partnership.

- Reverse missionaries – reassess approaches to mission in order to reach the host culture; focus on second-generation mission.

- Adopt a mentoring approach to leadership development – journey with others.

- Develop culturally intelligent leaders and churches.

- Develop third-culture youth and children's ministries that help them to negotiate their identity in multicultural churches where possible.